Collection of Acts of Kindness in War and Peace

UNBELIEVABLE ADVENTURES
of a WWII German War Bride

To Joanne

Angeborg M. Johnston

Jan. 2011

Ingeborg M. Johnston

LOVINGLY DEDICATED

TO

Jim the love of my life
and Master of Acts of Kindness,

My daughters Eileen and Jacqueline
as well as Beth and Will
all of whom continue to perform Acts of Kindness,

Carl my angel in need,
disguised as the "Computer Guy"

and to all of my readers
endeavoring to constantly perform
Acts of Kindness

TABLE OF CONTENTS

INTRODUCTION

All survivors have a story, This is my story, a story of survivor Ingeborg M. Balendat, beginning as a teenage nurse in war-torn Berlin at the end of World War II.

When I started writing this book, I did not have anything specific in mind. I proceeded because of the urging of Jim, my husband of thirty-three years, to write my life story and preserve my experiences for my daughters, my step-children, their children and the great-grandchildren. At the age of eighty-five, it is important to finish this task because I am the last living member of the German Balendat family and the only one to move to America.

As I continued writing and relaying segments of my life to Jim, my daughters, and friends, I heard over and over, "Inge, that is absolutely unbelievable!" The title of the book then became clear: "The Unbelievable Adventures of a World War II German War Bride!"

Through remembering thoughts and feelings, I transported myself back to the young woman who was experiencing every chapter and every story. It brought back emotions of past experiences to the point where I was writing and crying at the same time. I felt the terror and absolute horror of a war that I—as well as so many million others in the world—was caught up in.

I remember the glorious moment when I stepped off the plane in New York onto American soil. I actually felt the wonders of freedom under my feet. I came home—and I was free. It is hard for me to explain how overwhelmed I was.

When asked about coming home and feeling free, I usually describe two small scenes. Picture this: In Germany, if you saw a person walking down the street on both hands, spectators would gather watching. Their reactions would be, "Lock him up, he's crazy!" In America, those who watched the same scene would say, "Gee, look at that. I wonder if he's going to make it to the corner."

Here's another example: Imagine a woman wearing a red coat walking down a street in old Germany. It would encourage a few young people to follow her and loudly say, "Hey, old woman, look at you—wearing a red coat just like the young ones!"

I had such an experience on a bitterly cold day in January 1950 in Berlin. It was my first visit to Germany since I left in 1947. I was still young and traveling the first time as an American. I wore a beautiful, long coachman's coat—a gift from my loving in-laws for my trip back. I also wore that wonderful invention called "stadium boots." They were fur-lined boots that you could step into while wearing regular shoes. They were a godsend in cold climates. My clothing was nothing out of the ordinary to me, but I looked different enough to be harassed and followed for several blocks. I learned from that experience that the concept of freedom is looked at differently in different countries.

In my travels, I experienced the generosity and good nature that most Americans are known for and it has no likeness in the world. I wonder if that generosity built into most Americans is partly due to the big expanse and wide open spaces of the country. In any case, it is surely heaven on Earth to me.

Unfortunately, my observations show me that others take advantage of that generosity and good nature. As hard as it is, I try to understand these actions as coming from those who just do not know how to do things differently. Living in overcrowded conditions and never experiencing "wide open spaces," as one does in America, probably makes one think differently.

The close conditions in Europe, for instance, often cause people to look over their shoulders before uttering opinions. Constant encroachment in one's living space causes populations of whole countries to more or less close their minds and hearts to the world around them!

When I was young during the Hitler times, many of us did not believe in Hitler's ranting and ravings. We would defy his propagandistic signs, displayed in various places, whenever we could. Stopping at a pub with friends to dance after spending a day skiing the little hills around Berlin, we would dance the "swing" under a sign stating, "Swing tanzen verboten" (meaning, "Swing dancing is prohibited"). We also danced with our ski boots on , which was another "no-no." Most of the time our German parents and others would be shocked at such brazen misconduct.

We also disobeyed the signs on each table saying, "Eine Deutsche Frau raucht nicht" (meaning, "A German woman does not smoke"). Of course, we made a point of holding a smoldering cigarette between our fingers even though we did not smoke. It does not seem like much now, but in our war against the Hitler mentality at the time, it made us feel better.

I learned that habits acquired as a teenager generally stick with us throughout life. The awesome challenges of the war that followed required and build habits of survival. The challenges I met and still meet in my eighty five years of living have encouraged me to continue to approach and conquer them as needed. Those challenges over a lifetime created a series of what family and friends call my unbelievable adventures. This is my ongoing story filled with those unbelievable adventures.

CHAPTER 1:

Emergency Nurse Running through
Falling Bombs and Anti-Aircraft Splinters!

I, "Schwester Inge," had to run, duck, run! Take shelter then run, run again. Run as far as the bombing pattern permitted at that moment, repeating my efforts until I got to my post at the emergency first-aid station.

Bombs were hailing down relentlessly on Berlin, blanketing the city. The noise was deafening as the blocks and blocks of apartment houses collapsed, spewing bricks and concrete down on the streets, obstructing and demolishing them. Those were terribly frightening experiences especially to a young girl still in her teens.

Periodically, during a rare lull in the continuing, nerve-wracking noise of the bombings, I heard the incessant droning of the B-17 bombers as they flew over the stricken city in wave after wave, releasing their seemingly never-ending supply of bombs. The sky was blackened out by the countless bombers flying in tight formation, hour after hour.

Many times I saw a bomber that had been hit by German anti-aircraft fire trailing a plume of smoke, still trying to hold his position in formation. I used to say silent prayers for those brave young men in the stricken plane, doing the job assigned to them. I prayed that they could make it back home to England or be able to ditch safely in the North Sea.

Nurse Ingeborg Balendat in one-size-fits-all German Red Cross uniform during a quiet moment in Berlin

It was an ongoing ordeal for this Red Cross nurse (in Germany nurses were called "Schwester" or "sister") to report for duty at my emergency first aid station in Berlin. The formidable, ever-accelerating allied bombing in early 1944 is something I will never forget.

Yet, along with the never-ending bombings and the misery they created, I also remember that there were acts of kindness shown toward me during my daily or nightly run to the first aid station.

The air raid wardens were older or unfit to be drafted. They stationed themselves in front of apartment houses when the bombing patterns were not immediately above them, watching for fires. Spotting one, they took steps to douse it, thus preventing more immediate damage.

Because I had a regular pattern running from our apartment to the first aid station, the various wardens would be looking for me. Often one would run a little ways with me. One time I passed a warden who grabbed my hand and ran with me across a big, four-lane double intersection with bombed out streetcar tracks in the middle. It was a long distance to run, especially across and back—and *especially* while bombs were falling. We had to dodge obstacles and debris from destroyed buildings and demolished streets, and were grateful after we finally made it. This was an Act of kindness by a selfless soul, especially meaningful to me because he endangered his own life for my survival.

It was comforting to feel that warm hand holding mine. After a quick squeeze, he released my hand and went back to his post and I continued running alone. I so appreciated and remember those caring gestures, even after so many years have passed.

Russian Soldiers shelling Berlin already destroyed from British and American Bombings

On another occasion, I was not so fortunate. During one of my runs in pitch darkness, I got really scared, but I remembered what the supervising doctor at the shelter had told us: When you feel in danger, stop running and seek shelter.

I suddenly found myself all alone in the street. A bombing pattern had turned toward me and the bombs were falling closer and closer. The frantic shooting of the anti-aircraft guns following the bombers directed the increasing hail of hot, sharp shrapnel splinters to rain right down on me. It had gotten so dangerous that the wardens who would usually be standing outside apartment houses, watching for incendiaries, had all gone down into air raid shelters.

In the darkness, I felt my way along the walls of the nearest apartment house and found the large door of a big corner apartment house. As I ran through it, I thought I knew the layout of that building well enough to find my way in the darkness down to the air raid shelter.

It was even darker inside the foyer since the glow of the many fires illuminating the city was totally blocked out. I used my hands to guide me along the walls in the direction I thought the shelter would be.

I was wrong. My memory of the apartment house was more wishful thinking than fact. I found myself totally turned around and got more frightened by the minute. I walked back and forth, gliding my hands along the walls while bombs were falling nearer and nearer. I could not find an end, a corner, or a banister to guide me where I thought I should be going. I just stopped moving, not wanting to get lost further and become more confused. I slid my back down the nearest wall, sat down, and started to cry.

*More shelling of Berlin by Russian Soldiers. German civilians are
in shelters*

I sat there and prayed to God to listen as I asked for His help. "If this apartment house should get bombed, please let someone find me under the rubble." I was not afraid to die; I was just worried that my parents would not know where I was. I did not want them to go through life hoping, wondering, and worrying. They were already worried about their only son, my brother, Helmut. At that time, they only knew that he was one of the many young soldiers missing in Russia. I did not want them to have their only daughter missing as well, right near them in Berlin.

I could imagine my mother and dad following the path I took regularly to the emergency aid station, searching and wondering which pile of rubble I might be buried under, and how much did I suffer before I died.

When the bombing finally veered away leaving many more destroyed buildings in their wake, the wardens from the apartment house came up out of the bomb shelters and found one very bedraggled young nurse sitting on the floor, crying and so happy and relieved to see them. One of them took my hand and walked me all the way to the emergency aid station, delivering me to the doctor on duty.

The doctor in charge said that I had made the right decision. Every nurse on duty had to decide if it was at all possible to get to her post without endangering her own life. That decision, of course, made it much harder to staff the stations. We appreciated knowing that we had that option but also knowing how badly we were needed, we ran as much as ever—maybe just more cautiously.

A young mother had brought her two-year old daughter in. She looked like a little doll, all dressed up because her Daddy was expected to come home on furlough the next day. She and her mother had come to their Berlin apartment especially to be there to welcome Daddy home from the front. They had been living in the country, trying to avoid the bombings and perhaps feel a little safer where they were.

The little girl, without any apparent injuries, looked like she was sleeping. After the mother told us that her daughter was unconscious, and where the little girl had been, it was determined that she was probably the victim of an "air mine." That type of bomb was not an explosive one meant to bring buildings down; it was a high pressure device geared to explode above-ground, causing dramatic increased pressure designed to injure or destroy the lungs of anyone in its vicinity, leading to immediate death.

The heroic attempt by the doctor to revive her—with a shot right in the heart—was unsuccessful. I'll never forget her little face or the grieving young mother, having to face her husband alone the next day. She had to feel guilty that coming to Berlin out of love for her husband caused their little girl's death. What a burden to carry for the rest of her life.

Another instance I remember well involved a young Mongolian forced laborer who was brought in to the emergency station badly injured and bleeding profusely. I can still see his face in front of my eyes; he tried very hard not to be put onto the white sheets of the treatment table. With a pleading voice and gestures, he tried to tell me that he was too dirty and would make everything else dirty. I somehow managed to convince him to lie down.

Our intense efforts to squelch the bleeding were to no effect and the doctor told me to stay with him and comfort him as best I could because he would not live much longer.

That young man died in my arms. I'll remember him as long as I live, wondering who he was and where his family might be. They would never know that he died in Berlin, Germany, in the arms of a young German nurse called Inge.

There was no end to the countless other bombing victims that I attended while working hours way beyond what I thought were my limits.

As the war progressed, the air strikes were divided; the British would bomb during the night and the Americans during the day. Whenever planes were approaching Berlin, a radio station broadcasted warnings. Every household would keep tuned to the radio station twenty-four hours a day, as long as electricity was available. The radio stations broadcasted the sound of "ticks," nothing but ticks, like the ticking of a clock, all day long.

At night, the short time it took from the "tick...tick" stopping to the beginning of, "Attention...attention," people were out of bed half-awake, grabbing the most important things they had and were allowed to take into the shelter running down the stairs of their apartment house to the air raid shelter especially built in the basement of each apartment house with an emergency area on each adjoining wall which could be pushed in to permit people to escape to either side into the adjoining building should their apartment house sustain a directly hit.

My little dog, a white Spitz by the name of Kerlchen ("little fellow"), came running to me when he heard the tick, tick stop with his leash in his mouth, he was waiting to be stuffed into my briefcase.

I knew no animals were allowed in the air raid shelters because they might panic and hurt someone. However, Kerlchen was small enough to fit into the briefcase with his head sticking out of one side and the flap closed. I just could not leave him behind alone in the apartment after he already had survived a harrowing ride down on the flow of the rubble of a collapsing apartment house that had been bombed.

I would carry the briefcase, keeping my open coat draped over his head. He never uttered a sound, with all that noise and commotion going on. He was just happy to be close to me, feeling secure.

Kerlchen was a victim of bombings and "jumped" into my family's life. During one particularly bad air raid, bombs fell especially close to our apartment house, My dad and several other men from different apartment houses had just come back out of their air raid shelters, thinking the bombing pattern had moved away. They got into position to stand guard again watching for fires caused by the bombings when they heard the terrible noises of apartment houses collapsing close by in the next street. Before they could go to the aid of possible victims, around the corner at full speed came a little white fur ball that jumped at my dad, who automatically grabbed it and held on to whatever it might have been.

It turned out to be a little white dog, a Spitz that had to have been left by his owners in one of the just-bombed and collapsing apartments. Apparently, he got caught in one of the top apartments of his building and survived after being caught in the avalanche of rubble tumbling down four stories—along with bricks, furniture and all of the debris. He was unhurt but badly shaken-up and full of dust and particles. His family did not survive the bombing attack, and Kerlchen became my dog.

It was heart-wrenching for pet owners to leave their pets in the apartments every time they had to leave their pets to go into the air raid shelter but that was the established policy for safety reasons. Berliners had few pets left but the ones still alive were cherished and taken care of as best as possible

I had the good fortune to be able to take Kerlchen with me when I was transferred from Berlin to a wooded-area around Dannenwalde. I was the only female nurse at a "collection" camp for officers who had barely recovered from war injuries and were about to be re-assigned to fighting units. The camp also housed some thirty former art students from various schools and universities that were closed down because of the war. Quite a few of the girls were from my art school.

They were drafted into the Air Force to transpose films taken at night by spy planes onto maps. The reasoning was that art students had a good eye for detail and would be good for the intended jobs.

The students had a magnifying device in front of them, which looked somewhat like our monitors today, and marked the maps with the areas covered by these night photos. The maps would be cataloged and could be viewed on demand to see the terrain as troop movements were shifted back and forth.

My duties included overseeing the sick bay for the soldiers and the three medics running it and the separate sick bay area for the drafted female art students. The large room was dormitory style and located next to my quarters which was one of the four small corner rooms. The showers and restrooms were in an unattached barracks nearby. The kitchen and dining room were housed in a complex by itself.

I tried to visit my folks as often as I could but it got harder to travel to Berlin and back. (Various ways you got there-bike, tank, walk etc.) Telephoning got worse and worse as communication equipment was destroyed. At night there were few dimmed street lights that worked and of course when there was an air raid whatever lights worked were turned off.

Christmas 1944

I do not remember much about Christmas in Berlin in 1944 or in the camp. I know that most of Berlin had been reduced to rubble by American and British bombing raids starting in May 1940. No one knew how the war was going. Like most Berliners I was just surviving. Little did I know that on Christmas 1942 General Paulus's Sixth Army had been encircled on the Volga River by the Red Army where Hitler's mad scheme to rule the world started to fall apart. The long terrible retreat of the German soldiers in the cold bleak areas of the Russian Steppes commenced. I think this was about the time that Helmut became a Prisoner-of-War.

In the Spring of 1945 my mom, who was just a shadow of herself weight-wise and was mentally worn-out by the constant air raids and bombings. She came to stay with me for a few nights, wanting to sleep without air raids and get some rest. When she tried to return to Berlin after two days she could not get back. She was stopped by heavy fighting and was turned back by retreating German soldiers because Berlin was being encircled by the Russians.

High German Officials demanded that civilians stay in Berlin and fight

German civilians were to go into the streets and "Fight for the Father Land to the end" against the on-coming Russian hoards. I was stationed outside Berlin then. My Mutti at the time was with me but Pappi was in Berlin. He found a young boy waiting on a street corner for a Russian tank to show up. He was holding a bazooka (a weapon used to fight tanks). Pappi said he tore the weapon away from the kid grabbed him by the throat and told him to get lost and not come back

---

It was a blessing that she could not get back into Berlin. The facts showed that she missed the brutal treatment women received from the victorious Russian soldiers, who had unrestrained freedom to rape and kill for the first forty-eight hours or more of occupation.

I found out later that my Dad had put my-sister-in-law in a barrel and hammered it shut to protect her for that period of time.

Of course the German military authority dissolved. My camp like every German military installation was in a turmoil. Everyone scattered with ideas about how best to survive. A doctor I had worked with invited my mother and me to flee with him in the only ambulance as far as the gas would take us. We gratefully accepted and traveled in a northerly direction toward the American front line. There were four of us: the doctor, my mother, a rescued goat and me. We took what few possessions we could wear or carry. I did not wear my coat but put it in the back of the ambulance. We found out later that the goat had eaten part of my coat lining. Every one and every thing was hungry in Germany at that time!

As we proceeded north toward the American front, we came to a little town on the west side of the Elbe River and at the same time ran out of gas. Mom and I decided to stay there. We spent a few nights sleeping in the seats of a movie theatre and washing ourselves as best we could in the Women's Restroom. During the day I went from door-to-door in the little village until I found a kind soul to take us in. We found a young mother with her baby who did not want to stay alone in her apartment, wanting to move in with her parents. She asked us to move into the apartment and take care of it which we did gladly.

The young lady had taken her bed with her to her mom's house which left us with just one small bed. I slept on the bare floor cuddled in my rescued down comforter. It was a blessing to be young and fit enough to get through situations like that without any trouble.

Still in my nurse's uniform, I went to the hospital, offering my services. I was told that they had more nurses than they needed from defunct or destroyed medical units and hospitals, but would gladly feed my mother and me. We felt a great relief to have that assurance and thanked them for their kindness—another wartime act of kindness. At that moment, I felt discharged. I took off my dirty uniform and became a civilian again.

I was told later that act was the smartest thing I could have done in my whole life! Had I been captured in my Red Cross uniform, I would have been interred, interrogated and detained at an internment camp. My mother, who was timid, would have been totally lost and devastated without me.

I had taken most of my clothing and my fur coat with me when I left Berlin, trying to save as many of my belongings as I could. That is why I had my down comforter with me. The barracks I had lived in were not insulated and were cold, prompting me to bring it along at the time. Was I ever glad! My barracks room got so cold that the water in my washbasin formed ice when my little coal stove ran out of fuel toward morning.

My mother, who had anticipated visiting me for just a few days, was now with me indefinitely as we were waiting for the American troops to "liberate us" conquer and free us from the terrible Nazi regime. The warm winter clothing she was wearing was all she had. As time passed and the weather got warmer, she had nothing lighter to wear and no way to obtain anything else.

I took the blue and white checkered duvet off my comforter, took it apart, and sewed her by hand a dress with short sleeves and a "v" neckline, which she felt most comfortable with. To dress things up a little, I took a white handkerchief we had and used it to sew a collar to fit into the neckline. The dress was the hit of the village.

I had enough leftover material to sew a dress for me. I designed a sleeveless one with a full square collar going from front to back. I then used the white firm cord we had tied our belongings together with and sewed it in a pretty design onto the collar. Another fashion hit was born. My art training paid-off.. All that sewing by hand made my fingers sore and bloody, but it was worth it.

Knowing my dad was caught in the fierce fighting during the fall of Berlin was a constant worry to us. We did not know his fate nor did he know ours.

When people ask how I felt about the whole situation, I did not give it a thought other than, "What do we have to do next, where do we stay, and what do we eat?" We were fortunate to have found shelter and were assured of receiving most of our meals from the hospital, so we just waited for the American troops to come and liberate us.

It was quite a sight when the first American tank came thundering into town and stopped in the square, looking ominous with the big turret gun pointed at us. We just stood there waiting, with our hearts beating wildly, looking at that awesome monster. Nothing happened.

After a while, the hatch on top of the tank popped open and a helmet and eyes appeared. Then the soldier stuck his whole head out of the hatch and looked at us. When our group showed no aggression, he pushed himself all the way to a standing position as we continued to gather around to look at him.

Cautiously and little by little, everybody came to life and the happiness exploded! We all just about fell around the soldiers' necks since we were so glad to see them!

As far as we were concerned, at that moment our war ended! Just like that! From that moment on we waited happily for the war to end officially. We felt secure from the Russian troops. Little did we know at that time what Russia had in mind in regard to dividing Germany.

The next group of soldiers we saw were with the American 82nd Airborne Division, They occupied our little village. When I saw their MPs (Military Police) for the first time, I thought they were the most beautiful soldiers I had ever seen! They wore clean uniforms, white scarves, white gloves and white spats over soft-soled boots. It was a pleasure for us to watch them walk. We *saw* them walk but did not *hear* them. Both the German and Russian soldiers walked with hob-nailed boots and were very noisy!

CHAPTER 2:

Living in My Beloved Pre-War Berlin

It was high noon in Berlin, Germany, on September 20, 1924. The church bells in Greater Berlin were peeling their joyous sounds, welcoming me into the new world and convincing my mother, Magdalene Balendat, that Baby Ingeborg Magdalene Ursula, who had been born to the sound of music, would be a blessed, lucky little girl.

I grew up in East Berlin in an upper-middle-class, mostly blue-collar neighborhood. I lived at Kopernikus Strasse 21, on the top floor of a well-designed four-story apartment house with balconies and a good view for many blocks, looking left and right down the street.

My dad, Otto Balendat, was a hard worker and a good provider. Everything he owned or bought was high quality. The "L" shaped apartment we lived in was large and airy. From the front door, we entered a long, wide hallway that led to two bedrooms, a dining room and a living room known as a "Berliner Zimmer," which was a large room connecting the front to the back part of the apartment. It led to a shorter hallway with doors to a bathroom and then to the maid's "Kammer," which was the same size as the adjoining bathroom (a small room like that was called a "Kammer").

I was grateful for its existence and it became my little piece of heaven, where I could do as I wished.

I had many pictures of American movie stars like Shirley Temple, Robert Taylor, Nelson Eddy and Jeannette McDonald plastered all over my walls. I changed the pictures almost weekly. Little did I know then that I would someday become a proud American citizen myself.

My treasured room was large enough for a bed, a small wardrobe and a dresser/desk fitting under a narrow, tall window. The little room had no heat but hardly ever got cold. When it did , my dad would take my featherbed into the living room and hold it full-length against the big tile oven to warm it. I would jump into bed, waiting for him to come and cover me quickly with the warmed comforter.

The small hallway, with drawers and coat racks on each side of it, led to my "Kammer," and also to the adjoining bathroom with its big tub and toilet. Further on, it led to a big kitchen with a large, brick cooking stove and a brick oven for baking and roasting. Both were fired by brown coal. Attached to the brick stove was a four-burner gas stove. A pantry with a window and good ventilation was used to keep our food and vegetables fresh since we had no refrigeration.

A double window made the kitchen a pleasant place to be. The kitchen accommodated two nice-sized "Schraenke," floor-to-ceiling cabinets holding everyday dishes, pots, and silverware. A door in the kitchen led to a spiral staircase leading into the yard that we never used, which was also accessible from the other adjoining "L" shaped apartments, providing a second entry or exit. It also led to the back-yard, which faced the attached apartment buildings that were mirror images of our apartment house. The whole structure formed a large, square yard with patches of grass and trees.

Our apartment was considered progressive when it was built. Imagine having maids' quarters and a separate entrance and exit for the maid to use! It even had electric bell-buttons in each room to summon the maid. While we did not have a live-in maid, we did bring in outside household help.

The apartment was well furnished and the hardwood floors were carpeted with beautiful Oriental rugs in the living and dining rooms. Each room was heated by a large "Kachel Ofen," a tiled heater. It used brown coal and supplied sufficient heat even in the larger rooms. The area around the "Kachel Ofen" was called "Die warme Ecke"; this warm corner had upholstered chairs and a loveseat arranged close by. It was a popular, cozy spot to be used all through the winter.

We had a balcony spanning the width of our apartment, lead-ing into the dining room with its double window and French doors.

The balcony was transferred into a little outside garden every summer, with flower boxes filled with pink, hanging geraniums, which my mother planted and lovingly tended. She grew tomatoes and herbs every year. The floor of the balcony had a drain, making it easy to water the plants.

A retractable awning provided shade and shelter from sun and rain. The comfortable outdoor furniture created a delightful spot to sit and have the traditional "Kaffe" and "Kuchen" (coffee and cake) in the afternoons whenever time permitted. I have fond memories of growing up in that pleasant environment. In fact, Jim and I still follow that tradition of sitting on our deck in Oak Harbor on Whidbey Island, Washington, enjoying the beautiful, unobstructed view of the Puget Sound.

CHAPTER 3:

Alt Tucheband—My Grandparents'
Small Village Life

I remember my only set of grandparents very fondly; my mother's parents were Julius and Amanda Hildebrandt. They lived all their married life in a little village, Alt Tucheband, about a two-hour drive from Berlin, close to the Polish border in East Germany, about one hour by horse and carriage from the nearest railroad station. My grandfather was a "Baecker Meister," having completed the rigorous training to become a "master" baker.

How lucky I was to have been able to spend four weeks a year visiting my grandparents, my aunts, Kate and Grete, and my adoring Uncle Paul, who lived with his family a few houses down the road.

My parents raised both my brother and me to be close to the Hildebrandt family. They made sure we kept our grandparents as an active part of our family and encouraged us to understand and respect the older generation, living an entirely different lifestyle in such an entirely different world. We successfully merged "big city" and "tiny village" life. My grandparents never, and I mean never, left the village. They never had the desire, or maybe the courage, to venture out of their environment. We were taught to respect that.

> *Visiting Alt Ttucheband*
>
> *My mom said our car would drive into my grandparent's yard and within minutes my friends in all of Alt Tucheband would be there to welcome me back for a few weeks of fun! I played with the village children and formed good friendships until the turmoil of war ripped most of our lives apart.*

My big thrill each summer was getting—after much begging and some tears—leather-topped wooden clogs from the small shoemaker across from my grandparents' house. I was so proud to wear them, just like my friends did! After a rain, being able to walk through every puddle was very special and an adventure for me, the big city girl! My parents and grandparents did not like me to wear the clogs and thought them to be unbecoming. They did not share my enthusiasm, and I was never allowed to take them back to Berlin with me.

A few other fond summer memories include the Karussell, a two-seated merry-go-round that my Uncle Paul built for us out of wood. Two people would walk in the center, pushing the cross bars with the hanging seats to make it go around. We would all take turns pushing and riding. We had great fun sitting on a board that hung from the cross bars and enjoying the ride.

Another adventure for me was that two or three of my friends and I would sit in a big bathtub in the middle of the "Hof" (yard) and have lunch served on a tray. The tub would be half-filled since it was very deep. Otherwise we would have been submerged! Doesn't that sound like fun? For me as well as my friends, who would never have had the chance to experience something like that, it was a real treat.

I was a skinny little thing because I was not much of an eater. It seemed my grandfather fed my friends and the whole village good food and sweet rolls when they came to play with me, just to encourage me to eat! And they loved and appreciated it. To this day, I am still not much of an eater.

One of my other memories was being invited by the neighbors, the Andersons, to their dairy farm, and being treated by their two sons to various goodies and adventures. We milked the cows and aimed the stream of milk at each other. I usually got the brunt of the milk war since I had no expertise in milking and could not retaliate very well.

We rode on the big, beautiful horses, which looked like Anheuser-Busch horses, and climbed up into the pigeon loft to hold and look at the miniature, colorful pigeons. Being there made me feel so welcome.

Lucky me, when I visited my grandparents in the winter and there was snow on the ground, the Andersons would send their spectacular "one-horse, partly open sleigh," with bells, fur blankets, and treats, to the train station to pick me up. Riding in that sleigh with the bells chiming with every step the horse took was like a dream come true. How wonderful it is to remember such many diverse adventures!

My grandparents had one of the biggest houses in that little village. On one whole side of the house were the bedroom, living room and sitting/dining room for my grandparents. Their rooms adjoined the kitchen, with its stone floor and large, brick stove that was kept hot at all times, summer and winter. The other half of the building housed the bakery and the big, brick oven. In the front middle of the house was the large store with the shelves displaying all the different breads, rolls, and beautiful-looking pastries.

My grandfather was the main baker and, besides his son Paul, employed another baker, a pastry baker and an apprentice. My aunts drove a wagon with two horses several times a week to settlements around the village, delivering bread and pastries.

I remember that when the wagon came back from their route and the money was brought in and dumped on the large table, I was allowed to count the silver marks and pile them in tens on top of each other.

The bakers were housed on the second floor. Two men shared a bedroom, as I recall. A large center room on the second floor was my two aunts' bedroom and it had an adjoining room with four beds in it under the sloping roof, which was used just for us when we visited them.

On the second floor opposite the bedrooms was a large storage room for flour and grains with chutes supplying flour to the big mixing troughs below, where the baking was done. Beside that room was a large attic with functional sky lights for drying the laundry. The full basement was large and built with domed stone ceilings, as well as stone floors and walls. The basement area was divided into several rooms: one for storage of vegetables and fruits, always smelling so deliciously of the beautiful apples my grandmother grew; another area was designated as the laundry; and there was one special area to accommodate wine making.

I remember one time my parents thought that Helmut and I were getting sick because we acted so funny. Guess what? We were drunk because my grandmother let us taste the black currant wine she was famous for.

On the opposite side from my grandparents' sitting room on the first floor, mirroring that room, was a work room used for preparing the different breads, rolls, and pastries. The large "Backofen," the oven for baking, was in the middle of that area. Next to the oven was a room called the warm room, "warme Stube," that was used as a family room. All of us would gather there to eat our meals or just pass the time.

My grandfather would read every night after the evening meal out of a book of parables or the Bible. The evening meal, "Abenbrot" in German, consisted of various freshly baked breads accompanied by homemade sausages, cold cuts, ham, and bacon. The hard-boiled eggs were gathered from the family's own chickens.

I loved the Abenbrot time and always came home early from playing. I never wanted to miss the time when everyone got together in the evening at a large table to listen to my grandfather read. Even the employees joined us most of the time.

My grandfather looked just like von Hindenburg, the "Reichskanzler" (President) of Germany before Hitler came to power. He had white hair, which he wore in a crew cut, and sported a beautiful handlebar mustache. I adored him.

Every Sunday the family would walk to the little village church for services. I recall that the church was beautiful inside and out. Unfortunately, during the war, the Russians advancing through the village toward Berlin demolished it.

CHAPTER 4:

My Schooling in Berlin

My elementary and high schools were all-girl academies, that was common in those days. The schools were about an hour walk from our apartment. In the winter, we went to school in the dark and most of the time came home just before dark.

The German Education System is different than the one in the United States. When I was ten, I was eligible to go to high school. The tuition for high school was high and my parents had to pay for both my brother and me at the same time. For that reason, not many families in Berlin were able to afford high school educations for their children.

To be admitted to high school, we had to pass an entrance examination. I still remember parts of that exam and one segment especially stayed with me. We were ushered into a classroom with nothing to look at but a beautiful painting and were left there for half an hour with instructions to study it. After the instructor returned, we were taken individually into a room and questioned at great length as to what we remembered seeing in that painting.

What was the meaning of the painting? What did it show me? We were asked how many particular items we could recall having seen. This memory test really impressed me and I thought it was great fun (Little did I know at that time that I would attend art school, benefited by having done so by enabling me to become a legal resident of the City of Frankfurt after the war and later illustrated some of Jim's children's stories). The usual math, reading, and writing exams were not

My first day in elementary school. The tradition was to receive decorated cones filled with fruit and candy to sweeten the day.

as interesting to me as the memory test. I was so naïve and young, and was taking this exam just because my parents and Helmut told me I should. They thought it was a good idea.

It would not have bothered me had I not passed. I really did not understand what was at stake. Lucky for me the decision was out of my hands since I passed and so did my best friend, Uschi. All was well and my parents and brother were happy for me.

Those students who did not pass the exam were automatically enrolled into trade schools of their choice.

In the first year, I started to learn English; French was added when I turned twelve. My favorite subjects were art, religion, and physical education. I loved gym and because I was a good athlete, I became a "Vorturner" leader. There were only three leaders in my class of forty-one students: Margot (called Felix), Ursula (or Uschi), and I, all of whom became good friends and were the leaders of our class. Our job was to demonstrate what was demanded of us during each exercise.

My brother marveled that we were required to perform the same moves on the gym equipment as the boys. Girls performed on the rings, parallel bars, the one bar, the high bar, and with rope-climbing. The only difference was basically the amount of repetitions. If we could not push into a handstand on the parallel bars, we were permitted to use one elbow pushed into our side to support one arm. Uschi and I had to use our arm to get into a handstand. Only Margot could do it without that additional help.

Looking back, I finally figured out that something good did happen during Hitler's time. There were no fat kids in Germany because the population of the country seemed to be in some sort of training to produce youths that were definitely fit!

I am often asked how I stay so fit for my age. I believe it goes back to the wonderful foundation that the demanding physical fitness programs provided during my youth. I managed to remain in good physical condition, helped by my many activities with my daughters as they grew up and because of my Red Cross Water Safety volunteer efforts.

CHAPTER 5:

*Family Activities During the Nazi
Party Pre-War Build-Up*

One time, Jim and I visited my girlfriend Uschi in Berlin; she had gathered a few of our remaining classmates together at her house. Most of them were scattered all over the country with the division of East and West Germany. As we were talking and reminiscing, my long-time friend, Margot, whom we lovingly called "Felix," mentioned that my family was the only one out of a class of forty-eight to have owned a car.

I was surprised; had she not mentioned that, I would never have known or given it a thought. Felix could recite all of our classmates' last names, providing she could do it fast. To this day, she has a remarkable memory. Never will she forget to send greetings to Jim, whom she has seen only once almost thirty years ago, but will never forgot his name. Felix became a renowned physician behind the Iron Curtain. I still stay in touch with her by phone.

When I asked how she knew we had a car, she told me my brother came and picked me up every Friday after school and we left for Mueggelheim, a suburb of East Berlin, about an hour's drive from our Berlin apartment. We had a little summer house there. Later, it became my parents' retirement home when they gave up the Berlin apartment. I realized, after my talk with Margot, that we had been living in a middle-class neighborhood, but living an upper-class life.

My parents owned motorcycles and cars early in my life. It started with a motorcycle and afterwards a motorcycle with a sidecar attached (called a "Beiwagen"). When I was five years old in 1929, I remember sitting with my mom in the "Beiwagen" and watching the trucks pass by. How big and tall they seemed to be.

We owned two cars before the war broke out. One was a burgundy "Stoewer" and the other, a navy blue Mercedes convertible. Because gasoline was rationed, the Mercedes was not used at all and remained parked in the front of my dad's factory while the Stoewer was used daily. Our beautiful Mercedes was dismantled piece by piece by looters during the course of the war. All we were able to save were the two front chrome seats with the navy blue leather upholstered cushions. My parents used them during the whole war to sit on during air raids in the basement shelter of our apartment house basement. Surprisingly, no one bothered those seats all that time. I do not know what happened to them.

My brother had a motorcycle that he rode to school. He was drafted into the "Arbeitsdienst" (Forced Work Service) right out of high school. After finishing the mandatory year in the Arbeitsdienst, he was drafted into the Army. He decided, since the motorcycle was no more use to him, that he would give it to me as a gift. I loved it and kept it clean inside the factory but I never did get to ride it because we had no fuel. Eventually it was stolen.

Most Saturdays, my dad making some excuses took us out of school. Every Saturday the Nazis and Hitler Youth marched through the street carrying the flag with it's big swastika. My dad could not stand the sight of them and the constant drum beat accompanying the marchers made him furious.

Luck was with me again! My brother was four years older and deeply influenced by my dad's beliefs and opinions while I "flowed along" like water in a creek. Had they not kept forcefully explaining to me what was going on and how wrong things were politically, I most likely would have believed what the school taught us and everything the newspapers proclaimed about the importance of becoming and being a Nazi.

I enjoyed writing and once got a prize at school for an essay about an opera by Richard Wagner, "The Ring of the Niebelungen." Would you believe my prize was a cast iron silhouette of Hitler!

After school I ran as fast as I could to beat my dad home so he would not see my prize, the despised likeness of Hitler. It would have made him terribly angry! I made it home before he did and Mom and I tried our best to destroy the bust with a hammer. I do not remember what else we tried but nothing worked and with a big sigh of relief, we ended-up hiding it hurriedly among stored luggage in a closet. It stayed there and Mom and I forgot all about it.

The apartment house got bombed later and one side of our apartment was badly damaged. At that time, I was a Red Cross nurse attached to the Air Force and had been taken out of Berlin with my unit. because of the damage to our apartment my parents had to stay elsewhere until the apartment was shored up and secured. When they were permitted back into the apartment, guess what they found lying on top of the damaged areas of rubble? Hitler's bust! My dad could not believe a bust of Hitler was found in *his* home. All he said was, "What S.O.B. did this to me!?" My mom did not say a word and he never knew how it got there.

Maybe it was my luck again, urging me to believe my father and brother and follow their beliefs and examples. Their ranting and ravings convinced me to stay away from anything connected with Hitler and the Hitler Youth. My mom was timid and scared. She just went along with my dad's opinions and hoped for the best.

The Nazi Party vs. the Ruling Communist Party

Pappi and Helmut often talked furiously about the Nazi Party. I didn't pay much attention to them but now I know that they were right with their passionate opposition to the Nazi regime. Germany was going through a great depression in the late 1930's as was most of the world. Hitler's ranting about "A chicken in every pot" and "A car in every garage" sounded attractive to a population that was trying to get through a depression that the ruling Communist party did not or could not do much about.

As students, Uschi and I had lots of pressure in school to join the Hitler Youth. She, Helmut, and I were proof that not everybody *had* to join! It took some moxie and creativity on our part to stay out of the awful clutches of the Hitler Youth but we managed.

There were Hitler Youth leaders who were seniors ahead of us at school and were fanatically and aggressively promoting the Nazi party. Whenever we were cornered or confronted by one of them and questioned why we did not join, we told them we were looking at different groups and had not made our choice. When questioned by one group leader, we would say we were looking at another leader's group, etc. We kept the confusion going until no one bothered to ask anymore, assuming we had joined "the other group." And when we saw the "leaders" in the street, we ducked into apartment house doorways until they passed us. We are still laughing about that today.

Uschi's mother's opinions in opposition to the Hitler regime were as fierce as my dad's. We put the two of them together in a center room when the families got together so the neighbors could not hear them. The door to the stairway of my parents' apartment was upholstered with leather to deaden sound and avoid anyone listening in on us.

Our apartment house was conveniently located near subway and elevated train stations. The train network crossed all of Berlin and reached outlying suburbs. My dad's factory was located along the shore of the River Spree at the Oberbaum Bruecke in Berlin.

Our little summer house was located within the Berlin city limits in Mueggelheim, east of Berlin and a short distance from the suburb of Keopenick. It could still be reached by the electric "Stadtbahn" or City Train.

Mueggelheim adjoined two lakes, the Big and Little Mueggelsee. We enjoyed swimming in the clear water and taking walks regularly to the beautiful Big Mueggelsee. The house was not the usual summer house constructed for weekend use. It was built for year-long use. My parents planned for it to be their retirement home. It was a wonderful house for use on weekends and did become a great retirement home for them.

The house was constructed of bricks and stucco with a heavy red tile roof, and sat on a large wooded lot. It had a big glass-enclosed veranda, or what Americans would call a sunroom, that took-up the whole front of the house. It also had a kitchen with a root cellar, a bath with a shower, a small living room, and a bedroom. It was heated by a large tile heater, the famous German "Ofen," in the center of the house. It had to be stoked with special hard coal bricks.

The "Ofen" had a compartment for heating water or for different functions like baking apples or keeping food warm.

A large attic was left unfinished, intended for later expansion. The front of the property was enclosed with a beautifully constructed stone and wrought iron fence, equipped with two automatic gates an intercom, one for pedestrians and a larger one for cars. My dad was handy and took pride in being able to install and use the latest technology available. He was always tinkering.

A large garden plot was lovingly tended and provided my parents with fresh vegetables. Planted fruit trees supplied them with all the fruit they needed. Both parents lived there until they died. Because of limited space, my mother's coffin was buried on top of my dad's, which was the custom, at a picturesque little cemetery in Mueggelheim. The graves are still kept up and cared for.

We spent weekends in Mueggelheim. During the summer vacations we traveled throughout Germany but most of the time vacationed at the Baltic Sea in a little resort town called Misdroy, since the ocean air was good for my dad's asthma. Misdroy now belongs to Poland. I have many fond memories of our stays on the Baltic; the last time was in the summer of 1939. World War II broke out in September of that year.

I was proud of my Dad, Otto Balendat, a self-made businessman who founded and built a successful business rebuilding automobile, boat, and motorcycle engines. His factory was located in the eastern part of Berlin on the bank of the River Spree. His business sign proudly proclaimed:

Meister Otto Balendat
Praezisions Automobile Zylinder Schleiferei

("Master" Otto Balendat
Precision Automobile Cylinder Grinding" [Re-conditioning])

The factory building was heavily damaged during the World War II bombings of Berlin, and the business was relocated. We were lucky and able to save most of the heavy machinery and equipment. After the war, it would have been impossible for years to purchase the needed machinery like the ones rescued from the old building.

Through all the years of Hitler's regime, my dad had been an outspoken, tireless anti-Hitler and anti-Nazi party advocate. After the war, his feelings were just as adamant about the Communist party. My mother and I feared that there would be retaliation daily. How long would the Communist party tolerate dad's aggressive anti-Communist attitudes?

We found out in 1948 after I had left for America when the infamous Vopo ("Volks Polizei"), the People's or Volks Police, made their move. They ripped my dad out of bed in the middle of the night and hauled him off to prison. He was in prison for six months without knowing why he had been arrested. I had only been in America a few months when this happened.

My mom thought it best to keep my dad's arrest from me, knowing how close I was to him and how my temperament was like his. We had the same attitude and reactions to the Nazi doctrine and Communist party propaganda, and had frequent rebellious encounters with Communist party members. She knew how frustrated I would have been had I known what was going on and was not able to help my dad from America.

The state attorneys kept asking him the same questions over and over. Finally, my dad told them, "Since you don't like my answers, why don't you just tell me what I should say, so we can get this over with?"

To make a long story short, he was declared innocent but negligent. When the scrap metal dealer got caught smuggling the metal he had bought from my dad into West Berlin, the dealer had to reveal that one of the sources was my dad's company. My dad was declared negligent because he "should have watched where the scrap metal dealer took the metal."

Imagine having endured six months in prison, most of it in solitary confinement, because of having made a Communist party member mad. I had to be grateful! Six months in prison was one of the lesser punishments. It could have been absolutely disastrous, ending in a long-term imprisonment or even death.

When Dad was released, he received so many flowers at his homecoming that they overflowed the Berlin apartment. My feisty "Papa" had tackled Nazis and Communists alike, sometimes grabbing them by the throat and shaking them. He had been treading on thin ice for a long time. I am sorry I did not know what was going on but I am sure that was for the best.

CHAPTER 6:

Willie Balendat, Art, and Swimming

One of my fondest childhood memories as a youth was visiting my father's side of the Balendat family in Nieder Neuendorf at their summer house two hours from Berlin. The property was located on the bank of the Hafel River with one side bordering a picturesque canal leading into the Hafel. Under the watchful eye of my distant relative, whom I adored, admired, dearly loved, and called "Uncle Willie," I learned to swim and dive in the Hafel at the age of not quite five. I also got support from my brother, Helmut.

I am sure you will agree that their unique teaching method would not have been approved by parents or been successful with many five-year-old girls. Helmut and Uncle Willie would throw me out of a boat into the river; when I came up they would say, "Do like this" I guess I was doing something like the dog paddle, and I did like it. When I ran out of air, they pulled me back in. Asked if I wanted to do it again, I happily agreed and off I went, being tossed with great élan back into the river!

Nothing about the process worried me—it was just fun and games, and I loved it! I learned to swim and be totally at ease in and under the water. I guess it helped to have been a tomboy and have an older brother to compete with.

Many times during the summer, while visiting my grandparents in Alt Tucheband, my mom and I would bicycle to Kuestrin on the River

Oder, to a large public swimming area with life guards, a beach, sun decks, and changing booths. It was beautifully designed; the beach led to the water and gradually into the deep swimming part, which was jutting deep into the River Oder, known and feared by many for its fast current.

My timid mother, whom I lovingly called "Mutti," would not go into even the shallow part of the water because of the swift current already noticeably there. She, her sisters and brother and my dad did not know how to swim. They were all amazed that I was such a tomboy and fearless in the water.

That summer, I received my first set of Red Cross certificates—the "Frei-Schwimmer" certificate—before I turned five. It was unusual for anyone so young to be able to accomplish that. Usually the certificate programs started at age ten.

I was having a grand time swimming with and against the current while my mom watched me anxiously. When I wanted to get out of the water to maybe jump back in, I was a little surprised when she asked me, "Why don't you swim some more?" I did not give it a thought and being happy in the water I continued swimming. She did not tell me that the "Bademeister" (Lifeguard) was secretly timing me. He had told my Mom that I was a strong swimmer and could earn my first Red Cross Certificate without really trying.

When I finally got out of the water, I thought something was up when the lifeguard asked me to come up on the high diving board with him; he wanted to show me something. While we were standing on the board, I asked him, "Are you going to push me into the water?" I told him he did not have to; I would jump off the board by myself, and I did.

My mom was so afraid for me—standing there, watching and looking up at us—that she could hardly stand it. When I jumped into the water and came up smiling, she was glad but exhausted from just having watched the whole experience.

When Mutti and I bicycled back, I hardly needed my bike; I was practically flying I was so proud I got that certificate.

The following year, I had already planned ahead; Mutti and I bicycled again to Kuestrin to the "Bade Anstalt" (Swimming pool) to complete the second certificate, the "Fahrten Schwimmer" Certificate. I had to swim thirty minutes without touching anything or stopping. I knew what was expected of me and had no trouble finishing the required time.

The following year I had to swim forty-five minutes and received the final "Toten Kopf" (skeleton head) certificate and a skeleton patch to put on my swimsuit.

When I started high school, I thought it was funny when I had to go through all the certificates again at the ages of ten through fourteen because the gym teacher in charge did not know what to do with me while my classmates went through their courses. So I did it again. No big deal!

My big dream had always been to be accepted as a member of the famous Berliner NIXEN (Nymphs) Swim Club on the River Spree. It was another one of the many beautiful outdoor swimming clubs right in the city limits of Berlin. It was not as scenic and elaborate as some, but was close to where I lived in East Berlin.

I passed that club many times, always wanting to stop and watch the practice sessions from the bridge overlooking it. Finally, in 1941, my brother took me to enroll. Lo and behold, after being tested for my swimming ability, I was accepted! I came home with the big letter "N" to be sewn on the front of my swimsuit. Since I was so little, the treasured "N" covered my whole front, but I was so proud!

Can you guess what happened next? The accelerating war efforts closed all clubs and I never got my suit with the beautiful white "N" wet, nor got to swim for the club.

That was just one of many disappointing experiences, having been a teenager in a country about to go to war. Luckily, I paid little attention to that part of my life at the time. Life just kept hurrying along, presenting more important problems to overcome. Looking back, it would have been nice to know if I could have won a race or two. But would I have liked that experience as much as I thought I would?

At such a young age, I was very proud of being able to swim across the River Hafel with my brother and Uncle Willie at my side. I felt like a big girl and was proud to be asked to join them. While we were swimming across the river, Willie would take the time to dive under fully loaded barges going by. He would be waiting for us on the other side of the barge, while Helmut and I had to tread water and wait for them to pass.

These picturesque barges were the permanent homes of their owners, who were living aboard with all of their family members. They lived like Gypsies. Some barges had flower boxes overflowing with beautiful flowers, and on some, you could see their colorful laundry lustily blowing in the wind. The wife might be sitting outside peeling potatoes or doing other meal preparations, sometimes with a dog or two next to her. We always waved at each other.

Willie Balendat, who was born in January 1901 in Berlin, became a famous cartoonist, depicting everyday life of the common people of Berlin. He himself was called "A Typical Berliner," a real "Berlin Character." When Willie was parked in his taxi cab, waiting for a fare, he would sit on the running board and sketch everyday life around him.

The Balendat family was close-knit, consisting of a widowed mother, three sons, and a daughter. One son became a pastor and the rest of the siblings each owned a beautifully kept taxi cab. Willie was the protégé of a professor at the "Staatliche Kunsthochschule" (Fine Arts Academy), who was responsible for him receiving a scholarship to become an Artist. Willie became very well known for his cartoons in the large newspaper, *The Berliner Morgenpost*. As a cartoonist for the press, using the name "Willibald the Taxi Driver," he was "discovered" by the art world and became famous. Willie was offered and accepted a teaching job at the renowned "Akademie Der Bildenden Kuenste" (the University of Fine Arts) in Berlin.

A copy of one of cousin Willi Balendat paintings, showing a man painting a grey sky blue, his way of expressing the value of a positive attitude.

When he was offered a studio for his use at the Academy, he accepted gladly but also reluctantly. Willie Balendat taught there but was always very conscious of "speaking Berlinerisch," the typical low German Berlin dialect, and would absolutely refuse to lecture or speak when he was televised.

Willie died in September 1969 in Berlin. In his honor, the Rathaus-Gallery in Reinickendorf held a show of a selection of his unpublished 400 oil paintings, watercolors, and cartoons that he left to his estate. I have some of his paintings and a postcard of a painting, which I cherish.

The following is a biography printed off the Internet.
Berliner Biographien (B)
Balendat, Willi
* 20. Januar 1901 in Berlin
† 27. September 1969 in Berlin
Taxifahrer und Karikaturist
Der Sohn eines Weddinger Droschkenunternehmers und selbst Taxifahrer kannte Berlin aus dem »Effeff«. Von einem Professor der Staatlichen Kunsthochschule gefördert, erhielt er 1936 von der Stadt ein Stipendium zur Ausbildung als Pressezeichner. Nach Militärzeit und Gefangenschaft fuhr B. wieder Taxi und erlangte Popularität als Karikaturist bei der »Berliner Morgenpost«. Unter dem Pseudonym »Willibald, der Taxifahrer« karikierte B. Mitmenschen in der Zeit des wirtschaftlichen Aufschwungs. Eine Retrospektive in der Rathaus-Galerie Reinickendorf zeigte 1989 eine Auswahl von 400 Ölbildern, Aquarellen und Karikaturen aus seinem Nachlaß.

I loved my Uncle Willie dearly. Since I am the only one in the Balendat family with the artistic ability to draw, it is said my talent came from Willie Balendat. True or not, I am proud of it. I had the privilege to take classes at the Akademie Der Bildenden Kuenste during my art studies, and my goal was to become a costume designer and designer of sets for movies and theaters. However, all schools had been closed down during the war, and I missed finishing my degree by one year.

I received a letter at the beginning of 1947 notifying me that the school was re-opened again and inviting me to enroll to complete my studies. Too late! I was expecting my first child and was scheduled to leave Germany on May 6, 1947, for Philadelphia, Pennsylvania.

My daughter Eileen was born on July 31 in Philadelphia. As I became a mother and housewife, my life was full and happy—and my future was more important than my past.

I took some lessons again forty years later, in 1987, at the Denver Botanical Gardens in Denver, CO, freshening up my dormant skills doing botanical drawings, which I enjoyed and for which I received much acclaim.

I also illustrated a few of the fifty or so unpublished children's stories my husband has written. Maybe when I retire and stop working after thirty years as president and CEO of our distance learning schools (the National Institute of Nutritional Education [NINE], the American Health Science University [AHSU], and the Institute of American Health and Science, LLC), I can get back to drawing and designing. That sounds inviting to me and I look forward to that.

CHAPTER 7:

My Brother Helmut

I also was always very proud of my older brother, Helmut. He took life much more seriously than I did, so life was harder for him to handle. When he graduated from the Gymnasium, all of his report cards showed that he was an excellent student—but he refused to join the Hitler Youth! If Hitler had won the war, we, the Balendat family, would have been victims of our anti-Hitler beliefs.

As long as my brother lived, he used to say that because I was little and cute, things fell into my lap. I have to disagree with that. Maybe it was my outlook, attitude, or possibly just my luck! I had my dad's personality. We were both short and feisty, and pretty much unafraid of anything facing us. I never took Helmut's comments seriously or thought he meant them in a mean way. My mom said that when Helmut told me he was not going to play with me, I told him, "That's all right. I'll play with *you!*"

I just loved and adored him and tried to do as well as he did. If he jumped high, I tried to jump higher. If he swam across a river, I showed him I could swim across that river, too. I took it all in fun.

While in high school, Helmut belonged to a rowing club. He was the "Schlagman," or coxswain, for the crew. He set the pace of the four- and eight-man boats. I was so excited watching them from the shore and cheered for them wildly. When their boat won, I jumped for joy; when they lost, I was sad. I enjoyed going to the regattas. To me, it was a beautiful sight to see the boats approaching the finish line and recognizing them by the flash of colors on their oars.

I remember one regatta when one of the oarsmen in Helmut's shell had trouble with the rolling-seat jumping the track repeatedly. They were still ahead and it looked like a sure win since they were so close to the finish line.

When the roll-seat jumped the track again, the young man who was sitting on it took the seat and tossed it overboard.

I was shocked and could not believe it when the eight of them sat there and laughed and laughed—and, of course, consequently lost! I stood there and cried. A kind couple asked me what the matter was and if they could help. All I could do was sob and say, "My brother lost." I guessed that crew was not as competitive as I was as an eight-year-old.

I will never forget the great honor I received when I was asked by the president of the rowing club to be his partner and open the Christmas ball by dancing a waltz with him. I was only ten years old. He knew that I was able to waltz; I had been dancing since an early age. I even remember what I wore that evening: A sky blue, light wool material made into a "Haengerchen" (baby-doll) style dress. It was short and hung loosely from the shoulders down. I wore white tights, black patent leather shoes, and white gloves. My hair was honey-blond and naturally curly, falling below my shoulders. Later I danced with my dad, Helmut, and some of Helmut's friends. It was quite a night for me. Helmut was proud of me. That evening, I was treated like a princess, and felt like one.

Helmut's Struggles as a German Soldier

During the war, we were determined to preserve the business for Helmut, who became a prisoner of war in Russia in 1944, on the Eastern front. We did not know whether he was alive or dead until August of 1947.. The Russians had kept him working in the salt mines two years after the war was over in 1945. Suddenly, and with little warning, he arrived in Berlin.

My brother Helmut drafted out of High school and assigned to the Motor Pool of the German Army.

My mom had smuggled scraps of food that we as a family saved regularly and hid in the top part of our trash at our factory. She knew she was being watched by forced laborers and prisoners, who would come pretending to empty the trash and get what little food was left for them. My mom kept saying that maybe someone would do something kind in return for my brother. As it happened, her acts of kindness in Germany got a response with an act of kindness toward her son deep in Russia.

Helmut was fortunate and survived the unbelievably hard three years in prison. He was released after a female Russian doctor testified that he had broken an ankle, which was not healing well, and that his general physical condition was rendering him useless to continue working in the salt mines. Before he was released, he memorized as many names as he could of the men who were still being detained.

He was hoping when he got home to notify their families and let them know that their loved ones were alive when he left the prison camp. Many of those left were craftsmen who were useful to the Russians, and were probably never released. Because Helmut was listed as a college student he did not seem to be of much use to the Russians. Little did they know how much help he could have been to them!

CHAPTER 8:

Living in Berlin During the Time of Hitler

I was growing up happily in a nice environment and thought I was surely close to Heaven. However, that was marred by the political occurrences starting in the 1930s. I was six years old and Hitler's Nazi Party came slowly into power and encountering less and less opposition over the years from the weaker Communist party became more powerful.. The Communists, however, kept fighting back, creating many brutal scenes.

Because I was young at the time, most of the public happenings are a blur in my mind. My parents tried to protect my brother and me from ugly scenes by not putting us into situations where they were likely to happen. I do remember people being dragged out of their houses by the "Gestapo," the German police. They were beaten, verbally abused, arrested, and taken away by force.

I remember the Nazis and Hitler Youth marching in the streets, endlessly beating their drums. As they marched, they were on the lookout for people who did not salute the Nazi flag. Spotting them, they would break ranks and run to harass and beat the offenders. Mind you, young boys were taught to turn their parents in for whatever "crimes" they might have committed, were perceived to have committed. Something as simple as having listened to a foreign station on the radio was cause to be arrested!

I had a friend who qualified to participate in Hitler's dream of a pure Aryan race—the vision was to have all Germans become a "pure" race created by selective breeding. All blond and blue-eyed people were encouraged to mate and give the child to Hitler and Germany!

I saw that sweet little baby just before they planned to give it away. The mother was one of the drafted art students, a nice and well brought up young lady. I did not know if her parents knew about her plan or endorsed it.

I did not qualify to be considered for that "glorious honor" since I was short and petite, nor was I blue-eyed or a light blonde. The funny thing was that Aunt Kate and I were the only two in our whole family who were sort of blond, but no one was blue-eyed. Germans as a whole did not look like what Hitler had envisioned and had wanted to create. Hitler himself certainly did not fit his own dream picture.

I had my conformation in March of 1939, and my mother was convinced that the young Lutheran pastor was wearing riding boots (Officer's) under his habit, which offended her greatly.

That was also the time when all churches were closed and couples got married by placing their hands on Hitler's book, *Mein Kampf* ("My Fight"), because all Bibles had been hidden or confiscated. Later that year, all religious services were suspended as well.

Golden Pheasant's Fleeing Berlin near the final days of the war.

History tells us that the German civilian population in Berlin were a resolute bunch partly because that was their style, partly because the Nazi regime refused to allow them to leave legally though thousands did illegally and partly because there was no place to go. The Nazi military was another story. Members of the various Nazi military forces left in droves, legally and illegally. Those who received a "Three Day Pass," the "Privileged Ones" left legally and were called "Golden Pheasants" by those left behind. Most of the others who could get away just left.

My Confirmation Day, March 1939 at my Lutheran Church in Berlin. Six months before the war broke out.

CHAPTER 9:

The Berlin Wall Adventures—How
Two Worlds Were Separated

The Berlin Wall, created by the Communists and one of the most infamous structures of all times, had been slowly coming to life as early as 1958 and was in full bloom by 1960, tightly surrounding Berlin and keeping the "little island" of West Berlin separated from the rest of Western Germany and the rest of the world. Little did the East Germans in East Berlin know or comprehend how that wall would dictate their lives for the future 29 years.

A worker building the Berlin wall. Above him the sign proclaims that
no one has the intension to build a wall.

Helmut returned to the old home and the old business in East Berlin that was eventually behind the Iron Curtain. Our home and business was in East Berlin so we all ended up behind the Iron Curtain.

Returning home was wonderful for Helmut but he did not realize that he was going to be a prisoner again! The Berlin Wall created serious problems for the whole East German population. His favorite explanation was that he had been too cheap to buy a ticket for the elevated train when it was still possible to get to the Western part of Berlin. Statistics show that some 2 million East Germans moved into Western Germany and beyond after the war but before the Iron Curtain was established.

A communist soldier sitting on top of the Berlin wall at its start to make sure East Berliners do not try to escape.

Because of previous agreements made by the Big Four-England, France, Russia and the United States divided Germany into four sectors with Berlin being in the Russian Sector. Berlin which was in the Russian Sector was divided into East Berlin ruled by the Russians and West Berlin ruled by the other three countries. The Spree River at the

Oberbaum Bruecke would divide the Russian and American sectors. Our family business was right there on the "wrong side" in the Russian sector! That automatically forced Mom, Dad, and me to also be on the wrong side. If it had been just the apartment and our summer cottage caught in the Russian sector, we would have sacrificed them and left. However, it would be difficult for those not familiar with the options to understand what was entailed.

The writing on the wall says that 13,000 wives were separated from their husbands because of the wall.

My parents and I struggled to revive and rebuild the family business, a real challenge. The extreme destruction of Berlin, the monetary circumstances and devaluation of all currency, and the brutal conditions put upon us by the Communist government had to be dealt with all the time. It was our belief and hopes that Helmut was alive and would be released from a prisoner of war camp somewhere in Russia and come home. Those beliefs and prayers had to be kept alive at all costs! To keep holding on to them was one of the hardest commitments of our lives. Making it harder still for my parents was the fact that their only daughter left for America in 1947, before anything was known about Helmut or his whereabouts.

Statistics have borne out the brutal truth that German war casualties turned out to be far greater than feared. Out of my brother's graduating class of some forty students, only three survived.

The Berlin Wall was heavily fortified and constantly improved against possible escapes. Mines and more mines were added in "No Man's Land," the large, bare areas along the wall. Anti-tank barriers, barbed wire, broken glass, vicious dogs, and double guards were among the many obstacles used to prevent escapes. The guards were always in pairs because if one tried to escape, the other one and his family would be held accountable. Many escape attempts were made by East Germans: tunneling, the use of hidden compartments in vehicles, and disguises. Most of them were fatal but it did keep the world focused on the cruelty of the Berlin Wall.

Potsdamer Platz a very busy center of Berlin before and after the Berlin Wall was built became an absolute deserted area when the wall divided it.

Forty years went by with family members and loved ones separated by the Berlin Wall, even though some lived right adjoining the wall. I visited my East Berlin family and friends regularly, two or three times a year. The visits were always difficult because it was like going to visit a loved one in prison who wasn't allowed to leave, but I could leave any time. It almost always created hard feelings. Many comments a visitor would make just in conversation were often not welcomed because they meant nothing to individuals who could not speak freely.

CHAPTER 10:

*Our Family Business in Communist
East Berlin Behind the Iron Curtain*

My dad retired in 1970 and he and my mom gave up the Berlin apartment they had occupied for fifty some years and moved into the little weekend house in Mueggelheim on the outskirts of greater Berlin.

Helmut's ownership, ingenuity, and schooling made the family business grow and prosper. He also became a "Meister" like my dad—Master of his craft.

To clarify, "Ownership" of a business in Communist East Berlin was like talking about a dream, a non-existent commodity. Any privately owned business under a Communist regime was unfathomable. The first thought coming to mind would be that the owner of that well-functioning business *had* to be a big party member. Communist beliefs were that the people, the "Volk," owned everything, which actually translated to the Communist Government owning whatever there was to own.

If you were an owner of a business, you were a capitalist, and capitalism was not tolerated. And if you were an owner who was not a Communist or a party member, that was even more suspicious and unheard of, and that person was scrutinized and watched beyond description.

So how did my brother keep his business and stay in good graces with the Communists? Anyone familiar with Communist propaganda knows the slogans and red banners all across the streets proclaiming, "Production, Production" and more "Production"—the goal which all the "Genossen" (Comrades) should strive for! However, all the back-slapping and usage of those words could not achieve the heralded production. "Genosse" and "Comrade" have wonderful meanings when you would look them up in a dictionary—*except when they are used in the language of Communism*, where they are an insult to non-party members. To this day, I cringe when I hear either word.

My brother kept his employees for many years and never employed a Communist party member. How could he achieve that? If he employed someone new and it became apparent he was a Communist, he used their own approach and party slogan. If a Communist employee made a mistake, Helmut called it "sabotage."

When you were forced to hire someone and that person turned out to be a party member and most likely a spy, the mistakes made by that employee were being forcefully noted and were proclaimed to be sabotage against the production goal. The employee was dismissed and the owner of the business was actually shielded and blessed by the watchful Communist party, guarding its production goals.

The small family-owned automobile repair shops in Berlin and surrounding areas were having a hard time maintaining their credibility in the big production picture. They relied more and more on my brother's intelligence and ingenuity, which kept their productivity at a steady pace and thus kept them in business.

If he could not rebuild the engines they brought to him quickly enough, they could not keep the clients and, most likely, the party members happy. He came up with a very successful plan. Helmut, I am sure, was the only owner with a higher education who had achieved the "Abitur". Which would have put him into the third year of college in the USA. Than the war started in September 1939 and he got drafted. His life stopped and he did not begin to slowly live again until he was released from a prisoner of war camp near Leningrad which is now St. Petersburg.

He saw the necessity of gathering the small repair shops together and founded a co-op, where everyone put in an equal amount of money for operating capital. Helmut developed business plans and connections, and took over the responsibility to be the buyer of the necessary materials like pistons, piston rings, and other needed parts.

Weekly, he would drive his car, with a little trailer in the back, from Berlin to Leipzig in East Germany and pick up the needed parts. Then he would bring them back to Berlin to the building the co-op owned. They had hired a secretary in charge of the inventory and she kept things accountable and running smoothly.

What made the co-op successful was the business plan that Helmut developed. Every co-op member's repair shop would work exclusively for one month at a time on one make of car. For example, one month the focus would be the "Trabant" another month the "Wartburg." It would go on with different makes from month to month.

Every member pledged to keep pace with the other members regarding their "production" (there is the magic word again), which made the co-op successful and, above all, powerful.

Another weapon that my brother had to come up with was recognition by the Communist "Big shots" that he was the brain behind it all. On top of that, when he was being harassed and maybe threatened, he would just say, "Hey, fellows, this is all getting to be too much for me. Remember, I'm an invalid and I think my health is in jeopardy. I better quit."

That would usually take some pressure off him and the co-op. The Communists knew that without his guidance, the "productivity" was sure to diminish and maybe stop. The big Communists could not afford that because it would make them look bad.

He told me he certainly did not mean to climb to the top and get all that recognition to satisfy his ego. As far as he was concerned, his brainchild, the co-op, was a dire necessity to keep the government from swallowing up all of the small businesses, including his own. Its success kept them safe. He and the co-op members celebrated thirty years of existence in the Palast Hotel, the showcase of East Berlin, which was usually not available to the East Germans, only foreigners and diplomats. But an exception was made this time just for them.

When Helmut decided to retire, he invited us to Berlin to help him celebrate. He must have had a premonition. He died four years later.

It would have been easy to fly into West Berlin and walk through "Checkpoint Charlie," as I had done countless times over the years. Helmut, however, suggested flying in to the East German Airport, thus avoiding the usual harassment when walking across the border from West Berlin, pulling our suitcases behind us. This would have subjected us to being searched and questioned, especially because of the expected gifts we brought along.

We had no choice but to use a Communist Czechoslovakian airline. We flew to Prague and stayed a few days sightseeing, since Jim had never visited that city. It struck us as interesting that all tourist guides would only show us castles and talk about the old history as if the period from 1930 to 1985 never existed.

We attended a tourist attraction called "An Evening in Prague." All foreign guests were introduced during dinner and when we were introduced as Americans, we were booed, which offended the English visitors sitting with us, who apologized to us. It did not surprise us, though, since we previously had trouble getting waited on in restaurants, etc.

The entertainment provided by native folk dancers was beautiful. The band played a polka and Jim and I danced. We love to polka and were having a good time, when we were asked by the performers to change partners. I ended up being paired with one of the visiting German soccer ("Fussball") team members, who was a really good dancer. I smiled politely but did not reveal that I spoke German. My German partner and I ended up onstage and were given the honor of being the "Polka Queen and King" of the evening. I received a Czechoslovakian male doll and my partner a female one. Jim had looked all over for me before he saw me on the stage.

Days later, we took the Czechoslovakian airline into East Berlin. Helmut's suggestion was correct. We were welcomed at the airport as "guests" of East Germany and treated with great courtesy. We experienced none of the usual unpleasant hostility and scrutiny. Our suitcases were not opened or searched.

We stayed two weeks with Helmut and his wife, Helga, who hosted us with pride and pleasure. Jim got to see famous tourist sights in Potsdam and where the World War II peace treaty was signed by the four Allied powers at the famous Fredrick the Great's Palace, "Schloss Sanssouci" ("San Souci," meaning, "without worry"). He also enjoyed spending time viewing the famous Pergamont Museum in East Berlin, and we were treated to fantastic opera and theater productions. East Germany houses a lot of historic buildings and places.

When it was time to leave East Berlin, we, of course, chose the easier and shorter way to go to West Berlin and West Germany, which was through "Checkpoint Charlie." My brother helped us with our suitcases within about three blocks of the Communist border and its guards, where Helmut told us he could not go any closer to the checkpoint because the guards would shoot.

The border crossing was involved in heavy construction. Improvements were made continuously to make crossings more secure in order to prevent people from trying to leave "The Workers' Paradise."

As Jim and I approached the gate, we were stopped by one of the despised border guards. He gruffly asked for our passports and papers and barked at us that we were at the wrong gate—this one was for diplomats only. I told him in German that we did not know there was another gate. He glared at me and barked, "How come everyone else knows where to go and you do not?"

With the biggest smile I could muster, I looked right into his eyes and replied, "That is because we are both dumb." You should have seen his face—his expression was priceless! He grumbled and proceeded to take us just a few feet further to the "right" gate.

We were happy to be back in the Western atmosphere, where things were clean, public telephones were functioning, and people smiled. We were back in another world, our free world! However, it was always hard for me to walk away from my last family member imprisoned by a cruel government.

CHAPTER 11:

*How I Became a War Bride, Moving from
Berlin to Frankfurt and to the U.S.A.*

I had met an American serviceman, who I found out was a counter-intelligence agent, and who spoke German and French fluently. He was charming and we fell in love.

When he was shipped back to the States, all contact ceased since there was no mail service between Germany and the U.S. I had his address, and my girlfriend Uschi's American boyfriend agreed to send one letter to him. If he did not get an answer, he would not send anymore. Well, he got an answer...and we could correspond until he cam back to Germany as a civilian employee for the war department.

He was in charge of the railway freight shipment security and anti-looting around Frankfurt. His job included preventing loitering around the Frankfurt railway station and looting of the freight trains. It was a big job. In the course of events, we were invited to the home of the President of the German Railroad. In Germany, that was a big honor at the time. I think it was pleasant, but I do not remember much about those occasions.

Because of his having been a counter-intelligence agent, my fiancé could not come to Berlin in 1946. That left us with just one choice: I had to get to Frankfurt. The big question was: HOW?

I decided to get a knapsack and started off to the Russian border, attempting to get into the British sector. As we were all milling around the border town, I met and decided to join a man and two boys, who were also attempting to get across the border into the British sector to find his wife and the boys' mother.

Germany was totally destroyed and torn into so many pieces; people were just trying to find their families. Every house, every pole, and every wall had hundreds of notices plastered all over them, asking, "Have you seen my mother?" etc.

We decided to attempt the crossing at two o'clock in the morning. We crossed a stubble field, trying to make as little noise as we could manage. And no talking! We walked and walked and when we thought we were in the British sector, we started to whisper to each other. We misjudged and had not yet reached the British part. To our horror, we heard the dreaded "Stoy" ("Stop") screamed at us! Two Russian soldiers crawled out of stacked cornstalks and ran toward us with their rifles pointed at us. Well, we stopped with our hands up and pictures in our minds of being hauled away and put in prison!

The Russian soldiers looted our knapsacks of anything edible and drinkable then started getting aggressive with me, the only female, feeling my body and wanting to know how old I was. I wore a windbreaker with the hood tied tightly under my chin; I told them I was fifteen years old. As things were getting more uncomfortable, they separated me from the males, telling them to sit or they'd shoot. At that time, however, we saw a party of ten people coming quietly across the border from the British sector into the Russian one. You could just see that the Russian soldiers could not possibly forgo the loot that might have been in those knapsacks! We were told to sit down, be quiet, and not to run. They assured us they would shoot us if we disobeyed.

Off they ran toward that group, hollering, "Stoy! Stoy!" Ignoring all the threats of being shot, the boys grabbed my hands and the four of us ran as fast as we possibly could toward the British zone. I lost a shoe running and continued hobbling over the stubble field, not even feeling the pain or the loss of my shoe! We made it to the British sector without getting shot by the Russian guards, and we walked and walked until we found the railroad station. We got into the next train and made it to the American border.

At the border, when the freight train stopped, we heard, "Everybody out of the train with knapsacks and suitcases!"

With our hearts beating in our throats, we obeyed and stood behind our opened belongings. I'll never forget when I saw the most beautiful American MP I could have imagined, wearing a white scarf, white gloves, and white spats over his boots, coming down the line and asking everyone for travel papers.

When he got to me, since I did not have any papers, I just had to give him the love letter my fiancé had sent, explaining why he could not come to Berlin and I had to come to Frankfurt.

He read it, smiled, and said, "Get into that train!"

I sure understood him and moved fast, getting into the train and sitting there, waiting and praying for it to get moving! What a relief it was when the train finally started toward its next stop, Frankfurt.

I met with my fiancé and all was well. Since he had a "big shot" job, the German railroad liaison people had found a nice room for us on railroad property.

So far, so good! The next hurdle to overcome was that it was illegal to live in Frankfurt without being registered in order to receive ration stamps. The city required that you applied for legal residence.

I went through all of the required motions. When I was asked by the committee in charge of granting residency rights why I thought it was important for the City of Frankfurt to grant me legal residency. What would Frankfurt gain by my being a resident? Well, I persuaded them that, since I was an artist who had attended the famous Berlin Art Academy before the war, I could design clothing and coats for tailors who had no models or magazines to show to clients. Since no new materials were yet available, anything that could be ripped apart, re-used, or altered needed some pattern and design. The thick, gray wool army blankets made beautiful coats and checkered blue and white duvets made beautiful dresses. And not just that, but I could paint wooden boxes, platters, etc. to make gift items.

I convinced them and they ended up thinking it was a fantastic idea—and I became a legal resident of the City of Frankfurt. It really worked out well, too. I became successful and had a good time making friends, and my English improved. In the beginning of 1947, American GIs finally got permission to marry members of their former enemy. Wonderful! Fantastic! But this put me in an awkward position.

In order to get the required papers and background checks to get married, I had to go back to Berlin. The papers I needed included the official documents testifying that I and my family were not nor had ever been Nazis, that I had no criminal records, and that I did not use the ration points due to me in Berlin while I was living in Frankfurt.

What to do? With our connections with the railroad big shots, we found an older railroad engineer, who regularly drove a freight train into Berlin and back, to take the risk of smuggling me into and out of the city. If I had been caught by the Russians on that locomotive, he would have lost his job and we both would have faced imprisonment. Not just would he and I have suffered but the ripple effect would have spread to the engineers family as well as mine. As I write this, looking back, I am amazed what one does being young and foolish.

So off I went on another adventure. I stayed on the freight engine until we got to the British and Russian borders. The British border crossing took a short time, but the one crossing into the Russian sector took over two hours. The Russian soldiers searched everything, including pushing rods into the coal stored behind the engine to see if someone was hiding there. opening and searching the boxcars, as well as the top of and underneath the various cars in the train.

While this was going on, where was I? You would never guess! I was in a little coal shovel storage locker right next to the boiler door, where the fire was tended to feed steam to the engine. I was small, just about five feet and a hundred-plus pounds, so I had no trouble fitting into that locker. But I was cramped because it had to content with a low metal partition to keep the shovels standing upright. I had to slip in sideways with my head turned in one direction as I sat, sort of, on that partition. I swear I still have the grooves to prove it.

I had all kinds of thoughts running through my head during the first hour at the Russian border, while the soldiers made attempts to get that locker door open—luckily, to no avail. The engineer kept telling them, "Look, this is an old engine and there are no more keys." But communication was difficult.

The Russian soldiers spoke no German and the engineer and coal-passer spoke no Russian. They used hands, shoulder-shrugging, pointing, and head shaking to convince the Russians that there really were no keys! Their main focus was to get them away from the locker with me in it! The soldiers finally accepted the obvious: that the locker could not be opened. Luckily, no officers were present, for they, I am sure, would not have been fooled so easily.

There I was, half-sitting, half-standing, cramped, and vulnerable in that dark little locker, with just a crack of light showing through the side of the door. I listened to all the noise of pounding and rattling the door, and all the shouting! If they had found me, I would have faced an ugly future. Imprisonment would not have been the worst of it. To just get to the prison, I would have had to pass a long line of soldiers with "loving attentions and intentions!" I'm sure your imagination will paint a not-very-pretty picture of such an event.

I still bless the engineer who found the courage and the right moment to open the locker door—just long enough for me to stick out my head and turn it the other way to relieve my neck muscles—before he locked it up tight again.

Once we were in Russian territory, I had more freedom, but I kept hidden. I finally made it safely home to Berlin and even though we had informed my parents of our crazy plan, they could not believe that we did it. The other danger was that if I had been found, they would have had trouble convincing the feared Russian military police (known as GPU, and recognized by their infamous green hats) that they had no knowledge of my attempt. It would have been a terrible disaster for them and many others.

Waiting for the engineer to get me for the return trip to Frankfurt, I worked hard and fast to get my necessary papers together. I got it all done and waited at home, never leaving the house for fear of missing him. When he finally came, I closed my knapsack, thanked, hugged, and kissed my parents goodbye, and off I went—on my way to another adventure in the locker of the freight engine. Knowing what to expect made the return trip a little easier but, nevertheless, just as dangerous and scary as the first one!

I was permitted to come out of hiding the minute we left the Russian border. Being in British territory did not put me in any physical danger. The British would not have prosecuted me under the circumstances I was in.

When I looked out of the freight engine door, the British officer and soldiers who were escorting the train came running over the top of the freight cars to see me. They were delighted that I had put one over on the Russians and got away with it! What fun! We all sang "Goody, Goody by Me" all the way to Frankfurt.

The only ill effect I had from my adventure was the coal dust in my pores that I had a hard time getting rid of for weeks. Imagine all that was involved in my adventure! How could I have ever repaid so much kindness and help from so many people, risking so much on my behalf?

Fulfilling all the requirements for permission to get married was quite an adventure in itself. Looking back, doing that was harder on me than sitting in a dark locker on a freight engine!

I was led around in front of several high-ranking officers for inspection, like a prize animal. I am sure they all were nice people, but it did not change the fact that whenever I got nervous, I had trouble understanding English and what was said to me. That made the whole affair difficult for me, but I passed and survived that part as well.

The U.S. War Bride Act of 1945

I was unaware of the U.S. War Brides Act of 1945 that allowed spouses and adopted children of US military personnel to enter the U.S. after World War II. My husband Jerry was made aware of this when German Citizens were included in that War Brides Act and took steps to see that I would become one of the first German War Brides eligible to enter the United States. While most War Brides were transported by ship from Europe to the United States, I flew over. As it turned out I was told when going through immigration in New York in May 1947 that I was one of the first ten German War Brides to enter the United States.

I had a nice surprise after we moved to Colorado. We discovered that Colonel Duffner, who had given us the final permission to get married, lived at the Air Force Academy in Colorado Springs, not far from us. He was delighted to hear from us. We became good friends and saw him and his wife frequently.

Another adventure began when I was pregnant. I took the advice of my mother-in-law to have my child in America. Since Jerry and his family were naturalized, they felt strongly that we should help our child to become a true American. I am so glad we did! Naturalized citizens are usually fierce Americans because they know and appreciate the freedom and generosity of the American people.

Because I was expecting my first child, I flew to New York ahead of Jerry, who would come back home by ship and had resigned his position when we decided that our baby should be born on American soil. Most of the American war brides came across by ship as well.

My in-laws picked me up in New York and took me by train to Philadelphia, to their home. Coming from a war-torn, dark, and dirty country, I was overwhelmed by all the lights and all of the cleanliness everywhere! When we walked into their house, it was just beautiful and elegantly furnished. Jerry had never prepared me or told me what to expect.

I was given a tour and when I got upstairs, they showed me the bedroom and the bath that was to be ours alone. I was totally amazed! The colors, lights, and the pretty, plush toilet seat covers, rugs, and matching towels were just too much. I was overcome with emotion. I just sat down on that pretty toilet seat cover and cried.

When my in-laws opened the bedroom closet and showed me the maternity clothing they had bought for me, I felt I had come home— home to people I had never met before in my life! I vowed then that I would be a good daughter-in-law. And I was. I nursed both of them when they needed me, until they died.

Jerry and I bought a semi-detached house in a beautiful area in German Town, in back of a country club. What a pleasure it was for me to put my sweet little daughter in her buggy in the backyard for her naps in good air and sunshine.

My in-laws saw to it that their grandchild did not lack anything. You name it: furniture for her room, a highchair, and a play-pen. I had never seen a child's room so lovingly furnished. I was surely in heaven. Life went along pretty well after that, and Jerry's business prospered.

What a dramatic difference in the transition I made from a severely war-torn, dirty country where nothing worked and with few resources to begin the rebuilding process to a clean, fresh, country with unlimited resources. Never in my young life especially after enduring the hardships of war and destruction could I imagine that such a wonderful place could exist and that I was there to enjoy it.

CHAPTER 12:

My Bumpy Road to the First Mrs. America Contest

All was not as cozy as I first believed but then how could it be? Looking back, I realize that Jerry had "practiced and perfected" his pessimistic attitude and talked down to me all through our twenty-eight years of marriage—and he had done the same down-talking to both of our daughters.

When I had been in the U.S. for two years, we decided to sell our large house in Philadelphia because of the ever-escalating cost of oil to heat it, and to rent the top floor of a large triplex. Our landlord, Bill Gelrod, and his wife, Freda, lived below us on the second floor.

I have to interject that when we were looking for apartments at that time, rent control made them scarce and hard to get. After joining a long line of applicants for the Gelrod's apartments, we were told that they would call us. We said, "Well, so much for that" and went to the movies. When we got home, we had a message saying that we were selected to be the lucky applicants to get the apartment. When we went to sign the lease, Freda Gelrod remarked that she hoped we would not mind that they were Jewish. My husband answered, "I hope you do not mind that Inge is fresh from Germany."

> *My new country my new neighbors*
>
> *After WW II being a German War Bride and starting off in my new country I ended up living in an all-Jewish neighbor-hood. The doctor that delivered Eileen was also Jewish. As it turned out we got along fine and if it weren't for my loving neighbors helping me get an evening gown and assistance to get ready for the Mrs. Philadelphia contest I would not and could not have gotten involved*

By moving into that nice, airy two-bedroom apartment, I ended up living in a solid Jewish neighborhood with my neighbors proving to be my friends and accepting me with open arms! Freda and her husband became our good, lifelong friends, and were able to come to the wedding of the almost twenty-one-year-old Eileen, whom they had met and learned to love as a little two-year-old charmer.

When TV came to Philadelphia in 1949, our landlady invited us to come down to watch a show with them, since we did not have a TV set. As we were watching, a message flashed across the screen saying, "Any married woman is invited to interview to enter the very first Mrs. America Contest." The ad proceeded to give directions to a modeling school located in a beautiful downtown Philadelphia hotel.

As we were sitting there waiting for the show to continue, my husband turned to me and said in a derogatory tone, "Ha-ha, Inge, you could not even pass the interview!"

Well! I sat up straight and said, "Oh, yeah?"

The next day, I took a fairly new white pillowcase, ripped it apart, and used that material to sew myself an off-the-shoulder blouse. A while back, for thirty-five cents, I had bought a remnant of white material with small, red polka dots for a skirt. This was the perfect time to sew that skirt to go with my new white blouse.

My naturally curly, ash-blond hair came just below my shoulders. I was so fortunate to have naturally curly hair and all I had to do was wash it and let it dry to make it look like I came from the beauty parlor. It was July and I was nicely tanned from being outdoors with my two-year-old tow-headed daughter, Eileen. I hardly ever wore lipstick and never any makeup.

I dressed in my off-the-shoulder blouse, cute skirt, and red sandals. I wore no stockings. Freda offered to keep Eileen while I went to the interview. She also let me borrow a red purse to complement my sandals and the polka dots in the skirt.

On Monday morning, off I went by trolley car to downtown Philadelphia. I found the hotel and my way up to the modeling agency that was hosting the interview. I entered a large, long room with an imposingly long runway in the center and a row of chairs on each side, occupied with beautiful women, most of whom were heavily made up. I was twenty-four years old and a novice at what I was attempting to do. I found out later that most of the contestants were trying to break into show business and hoping this contest would help them accomplish that.

There I was, a war bride from Germany, just two years and two months in America, with no other motive than to prove to my husband that I could pass an interview! It was a dare that got me there!

I sat down in the only vacant chair at the end of the runway. While waiting my turn to be called, I enjoyed myself and studied the waiting contestants. I thought I was in a funny situation, sitting there, wondering about the motives of each of the other participants. What brought them here? Studying other contestants vying to become Mrs. Philadelphia and maybe Mrs. America, I mentally selected several and gave them my vote of approval. Others I felt were way out of their league. All were taller than my five-feet, and more than my hundred pounds in weight. I had no expectations and nothing was at stake for me. I was relaxed and enjoying my newest adventure.

At the end of the runway was a Spanish screen behind which everyone that had been called disappeared. I became more and more curious about what was going on. As time passed, I noticed that ever so often, men's heads would pop up from behind the screen and look at me. It struck me as very odd.

When it was my turn for the interview, I faced four men and a lady. They questioned me and, toward the end, one man asked me to lift my skirt and show my legs. It was the first time in my life that I had been asked by some stranger to pull up my skirt and show my legs! Being in a bathing suit or shorts with bare legs was different and no big deal, but being asked to lift my skirt by four men (the lady did not bother me) sure put a different spin on the situation at the time. After a few more questions, I was dismissed with, "We'll call you."

I got back on my trolley car and went home. My husband said, "Well? Did you make it?" I told him we just had to wait and see, but I had the feeling that I had a chance. That Monday evening, I was called and told that I was chosen to be on television on Wednesday. It was two days' notice!

What a surprise to suddenly be required to have an evening gown, a bathing suit, and to act like a model! My neighbors looked into all their closets and boxes and came up with an old, strapless, black taffeta gown with little gold circles appliquéd. Some of the circles had fallen off but that did not bother me and we ignored it.

The next day, I again took the trolley car and went to Philadelphia to Gimbel's Department Store's bargain basement and bought a royal blue swimsuit with one strap across my shoulder for a dollar-fifty. It was just beautiful!

(Much later, at the beach, I experienced pure terror when I went into the ocean for the first time and my suit got wet. The material got so large, wide, and stiff that I could not get out of the water because people lying in the sand could have looked straight up and right through from the bottom all the way out the top. Jerry had to bring a towel to wrap around me.)

When I came home from the store, my nice neighbors fitted the taffeta dress to my figure and it did look nice. They did all that in one day, between the interview and the actual TV appearance. My German-Jewish doctor, who had immigrated to the U.S. in 1938 and had delivered Eileen, was so excited about my appearance in that contest that he closed his office for the time that I was to appear on television. You can imagine how grateful I felt that people could put religious differences and nationalities aside and enjoy my experience with me.

My little daughter Eileen was watching TV with our landlady. When she saw me on the TV screen, she jumped up and down and kept saying, "That's my mommy."

What made my being on television even funnier was that I was so short, and the old black and white TVs distorted people's appearances and made me look even shorter than I was and very squat! Besides that, my tan made me look very dark! I looked much darker than my skin really was. The whole thing was hilarious.

The bathing suit competition was the first part. When I was announced, walking through an arch of flowers, as "beautiful Mrs.," I had a hard time not bursting out laughing. I guess beauty does lie in the eyes of the beholder! I had to pose and model my pretty dollar-fifty bargain basement swimsuit with the camera zooming in on various parts of me. What fun!

The second part was the evening gown competition. I was awed! You should have seen the fantastic gowns the other contestants wore. I had never even seen such beautiful dresses before this contest. There I was, in my second-hand, black, strapless taffeta gown, which had been lovingly given to and fitted for me, making me feel like Cinderella for one day.

The third part was the "talent" competition. I had sewn mother and daughter sundresses, of my own design, made out of inexpensive material, which turned out to be cute and well received. I had never gotten used to the humidity and heat in Philadelphia, and had made these dresses out of necessity long before the contest.

The heat bothered our whole family and the three of us would go to an air-conditioned movie just to cool off; when Eileen got tired, she would sleep lying across our laps. When her "Oma" (grandmother) asked one day, "Eileen, what movie did you see?" she answered, "Baby swimming!" That baby was Esther Williams, getting famous in the movies with her synchronized swimming shows.

The fourth part of the contest was some sort of homemaker duties. I chose to make a strawberry short cake decorated with whipping cream, for which I used "Ready Whip." I did not know anything about marketing then but, as it happened, "Ready Whip" was one of the sponsors and I believe it started its production of that product the same year as the first Mrs. America Contest.

Another one of my "funny" moments in that whole TV adventure was when, after I put the Ready Whip Cream on the short cake and walked over to my place, the camera zoomed in on the cake to show how beautiful it was. However, the short time between my spraying the cream on the cake and my walk to my designated spot was all it took for the Ready Whip to collapse, making the short cake look like a blob of something I could not even describe. I thought I had never seen such an ugly sight in my life.

It was another one of my successful efforts in self-control not to laugh out loud! It was a blessing for me to be able to see the humor in all of this. I was only participating because of a dare; having come this far was just a fantastic and unexpected experience and would have been enough for me right then.

But it did not end with all of my fun experience! Would you believe, I won! I did not think that could happen and had not even given it a thought.

After all the excitement died down over my winning, I was told I now had to go to Atlantic City to compete in the Mrs. America contest. I asked, "Does it make any difference that I am not an American citizen? I have been in this country only two years and two months to this date."

Well, all went quiet! It did make a difference!

My runner-up, the buyer of women's clothing at Gimbel's Department Store, took over the title and I was happy to go home to my little Eileen, to my ordinary life, and to my friends in the neighborhood.

In addition to having had the experience of a lifetime, I received nice gifts. I was given my first orchid, which I thought was the most beautiful flower I had ever seen. In addition, I received a year's supply of Ready Whip. I loved that and made good use of it but made sure it was eaten right after it was applied to whatever I served. The big gift was that I was also the recipient of a wardrobe!

I had to go to the manufacturer's office and see the president of the company. Eileen, my cute little two-year-old with the outgoing personality of a ten-year-old, and I, wearing our mother-daughter dresses, took the trolley car and went downtown Philadelphia.

As she sat at the window like a little lady, trying to look out, she started crying. I asked her, "What's wrong?" and she told me, "The bad trolley car is 'hitting' me."

I realized that the tracks and the street were so rough that it was causing her head to keep banging on the side of the window. I explained what was happening and that it was not the fault of the trolley car. That was only the second time she had ridden in one.

When we were warmly greeted by the receptionist and ushered into the office of the president, he came toward us with outstretched hands, telling me, "I have been waiting for you." I was surprised that he would make such a fuss over me.

As it turned out, all his clothing started at misses size 10, and I wore a 4 or 6. When he had seen me at the contest, he knew that his line of clothing had nothing to fit me. That was the reason he made such a fuss over me, because I did not fit into my "prize!" I assured him that it was all right, I did not mind. Feeling badly, he offered me material to have some dresses made for me.

I told him, "I'd be happy to just get the material because I'll send it to my mother in Berlin, who still has nothing much to wear." Even four years after the war, it was still very dismal in so many respects.

You would have thought I had given him the biggest gift ever. He was so relieved to be able to give me something to make me happy. He had been worrying about my being so small and having to disappoint me by not being able to give me the promised wardrobe.

Not only did he give material for several dresses, but also material suitable for several suits, including necessary zippers, matching thread, and buttons! He was so generous that he even paid for the postage for that "care package" to Berlin, Germany. My mom was delighted and thankful for his generosity, and sent him a thank-you letter and a token gift from Berlin.

I was grateful for the unbelievable and unexpectedly delightful experience to compete in the Mrs. Philadelphia contest that came about just because of a dare. All my life I have been thanking God daily for all of the blessings He has continued to shower upon me. During the many years I have lived in America. I have tried and continue to show my appreciation and gratefulness for becoming an American by trying to give back to this country more than I receive.

I urge all of you reading this book to become aware of and to perform unsolicited and unexpected acts of kindness for your fellow travelers on this Earth! You will experience unbelievable results and gifts that will be given to you in return! Share one with me. www.ww2warbride.com

CHAPTER 13:

Look out, Colorado, Here We Come!

Soon afterward, a big decision came along that changed our lives. Jerry's allergies were getting so severe that they interfered with his daily life and work. Doctors suggested that he take a vacation in Colorado to see if that dry air would help his allergies. We did and it seemed to agree with him, so we moved to Colorado in 1950.

He made favorable business connections and we proceeded to build a good life. Jerry continued with his appraisal business and added a general contractor's license to his credentials. With the cooperation of our new friend and architect, Roland Wilson, I took over all construction supervision. Daily, I was at the construction site at 6:00 a.m., coordinating the work and the various sub-contractors with our construction supervisor. I was always back again at five o'clock to see that the site was safely shut down for the night.

A female in the construction field in the 1950s (and into '70s) was rare. And one who always looked like a female, even more so. I had the cooperation and respect from the inspectors and the various subcontractors and we worked all well together.

Besides the construction supervision, I was active in school affairs and was on the principal's advisory board of Eileen's school. After he once came to see me on the job, supervising the pouring of concrete work, he was so impressed that he wanted to get me on the TV show, *What's My Line?*, where celebrities tried to guess what a person's profession was. He was positive that no one would guess my job, and was sincerely disappointed when I could not find the time away from supervising our construction to fly to New York.

Besides my work, I was also active as a Red Cross Water Safety Instructor and a Red Cross Handicapped Swimming Instructor, plus caring for my family and being available to attend to my daughter's school activities.

Daughters Eileen and Jacqueline in 1958 in Littleton, Colorado

Daughters Eileen and Jacqueline in 2009.

I was living my American dream in the things I was doing and enjoying every moment of it. My memories of the war that were still constantly with me were at least fading. I did not wake up anymore during the night from a deep sleep when a fire engine would go by with its sirens blaring and dive under the bed. Every time I visited my mother and brother in East Berlin I wondered about what my life would have been like if I had stayed in Germany.

I would have probably remained in Berlin, behind the Wall at least until it came down. I would have tried to complete my schooling as a costume designer for movies and theatre. After that I don't know. I had friends and family in the East and in the West. I would have wanted to support my dad and the family business in East Berlin but I had friends and relatives, both important to me, in West Berlin and West Germany.

I would have found the extreme restrictions living in East Berlin especially troublesome. The potential to use the costume and set design skills I learned in art school would have been much more useful in Western Germany then in Eastern Germany. I now know that the creative juices in my veins would have flowed much more freely in the West than in the East.

My life always seemed to have a flow and looking back I am extremely happy it flowed the way it did.

Observations on Acts of Kindness

As Inge's spouse for the past 33 years I helped to gather information for this book from various sources. I was truly amazed at the volume. In Littleton, Colorado for example, Inge brought-up daughters Eileen and Jacqueline, helped raise thousands of dollars for United Way and took on various other projects for the schools, taught swimming especially to the handicapped, again raised funds for many other non-profit organizations and other miscellaneous activities. She has piles of Thank You letters written to her in different languages, expressions of appreciation for various projects and old newspaper articles with photos written about her good works.

James R. Johnston

CHAPTER 14:

*Denver Was Growing and so
Was Our Construction Business*

Jerry and I continued to prosper building and selling houses. We built a very modern four-story, fifty-unit, pre-stress apartment building with a swimming pool and recreation facilities. It was one of three pre-stress buildings being constructed in Denver at that time. Pre-stress was just coming on the market and was favored for building large units and valued for its sound-proofing abilities.

"Pre-stressed concrete" was produced by pouring individual custom designed sections, pouring concrete over reinforcement bars being power stretched, and holding that position until the concrete set. It was intricate work. Sometimes we would find the bathroom openings for the toilets and bathtubs in the wrong places and the sections would have to be removed and re-manufactured. However, we had no problem selling the units immediately upon completion and we made a good profit.

I also supervised building an animal hospital, which was fun. In addition, we built (and I supervised the building of) a challenging contemporary office building. I had a trying relationship with four different architects working on that job: one architect for construction, one for engineering and technical issues, one for electric and plumbing, and one for the custom inside build-ins and partitions.

That job was a pain from the beginning to the end. The "plumbing expert architect" tried to make the waste water flow uphill, even though our old, experienced plumbing contractor vigorously objected to his plans.

I had learned to listen to experienced craftsmen early on in my building career before accepting the opinion of a young, inexperienced architect. But that architectural firm was the "power" in that debate and the owner was somehow obligated to give them the go-ahead against our objections. We ended up with an expensive, all-quality, contemporary building, except for the need to use sump pumps that should have been unnecessary.

I finished my building career by supervising the building of three eighteen-unit apartment houses for us personally. It was my pleasure being the boss in that adventure. I supervised not only the construction, but I also had fun decorating the finished units, using four different colors in appliances that were just coming on the market. What made the picture perfect was that we were able to carpet each unit, matching the colors of the appliances. We were the first ones using that appealing concept of color in Denver. We had people standing in line to rent those units even before we received our permit of occupancy.

The sign I put next to the entrances proclaimed: "We are Happily Filled—No Vacancy." With the help of good resident managers, I managed those units until I sold the last one in 1980. My training in art all those years ago came in handy and fueled my imagination.

CHAPTER 15:

Daughter Jacqueline, a "Chip off the Old Block"

When Jacqueline was born on March 10, 1954, Eileen's fervent wish for a sister became a reality. All during the waiting period, she would say, "I hope it's a girl" and I would respond, "Even if it's a boy, we will love whatever we are given." After a big sigh, an "okay," and another sigh, she would look at me before walking away and say, "I still hope it will be a girl!"

Jacque, being the youngest daughter by seven years, had all the advantages of an only child. I took her with me wherever I went, whatever I was doing—just as I had taken Eileen along when she was the only child.

The two girls and I were more in the water than out. Jacque learned swimming from the day she was born. She was already standing in the White Sands Lake, a private swim club in Denver, when she was three months old. As she grew older, the level of her activities grew along with her and fit right into the pattern of the family activities.

Jacqueline was with me everywhere I went

When I taught life-saving classes out in the White Sands Beach Lake, off a raft, she would hold on to my shoulders as I was swimming with my class to the raft, then just sit on the raft and watch the class.

When we all swam back, Jacqueline again held on to my shoulders to get back to shore. As she grew and her skills and stamina increased, she would swim toward the raft as far as she could go and if she needed to catch her breath, she would hold on to me again. No big deal for her. Growing up being around and in swimming pools so much, she became a competent swimmer already at the age of four. She just loved it and qualified to swim for the University of Denver's Hill Topper swim team at four-and-a-half joining another four and a half year old with three sisters swimming for the Hiltoppers. She became a member of Eileen's swim team. Eileen was also a member of the Hilltoppers Diving team.

The starter blocks were taller than Jacque. She became quite a competitor, winning a lot of blue ribbons and team awards all through elementary school. Her suit was so small that the many patches the team won did not fit up and down in one row on the left side of her swimsuit, like her teammates' did. She had to have two rows next to each other. (Jacque, now fifty-six years old, still has that little suit and her University of Denver team sweat jacket, with her number on it, that I had saved for her.)

After completion of our pool in March of 1958, it was being filled for the very first time and Jacque was around it with a little butterfly net, trying to catch bugs in the water when she fell in. Eileen was working on a science fair project with planarian, carnivorous flatworms. She needed bugs to feed them and Jacque was trying to help.

The weather in Colorado was still cool at that time of year and she was dressed warmly, wearing cowboy boots, a cowboy hat, and a parka. The water in the pool running straight out of the hose was cold and the March sun did not have much warmth. The pool had a heater but it could not be used until the pool was completely filled.

Eileen was in her room overlooking the pool, doing homework. I was working in the kitchen at the front of the house when she called to me, "Mom, Mom, Jacque just fell into the pool!"

When we ran downstairs, Jacque had already climbed out of the pool. We had to laugh! Just picture this: There stood that skinny, little girl, shivering, holding her container and the butterfly net, which she never lost. Water was running out of her pockets and flowing out of her cowboy boots, but she looked at us and said, "Don't worry! I only fell in a little bit."

Our neighbor, Milt Heisner, who was trimming his bushes, heard and saw her fall in. He was laughing so hard that he could hardly speak. He kept saying, "How does one fall into a pool's deep end 'just a little bit'?"

I had impressed on Jacque that should she ever fall into deep water, when coming up, she should turn on her back and look around to see where she should swim to. She said to me, "Mom, I could not turn on my back because my boots kept pulling me down. I had to swim out."

Because of our lifestyle and activities, we were good examples to other families, friends, and strangers. My friend, who had a teenager who was swimming competitively and repeatedly getting close to winning but just not making it, persuaded me to come to a meet and watch her son swim. I was to analyze what was wrong and help him, whatever it took.

I agreed to join the parents and watch their son swim the backstroke. Jon was a tall, powerful, young boy with love for competition and the water. What I saw at that meet were common mistakes made by many swimmers. One mistake was a very simple one: He dragged his bottom while swimming the backstroke. His second mistake was, just before touching the finish mark while swimming the breast stroke, he'd pull both hands back before finally reaching for the wall. Just a split second, but enough to be "out touched."

After the meet we talked and set up some sessions and worked on that. The next meet, his parents and I watched him swim again. He started to swim the backstroke and would you know it, dragged his bottom! Before we could even remark on that between us, he suddenly snapped to it, pulled up his bottom, stretched way back, and became as fast as an arrow. He WON! What fun that was! It became his best stroke from then on! And he won the breast stroke in that meet, too. That day, he got his first two blue ribbons and came running to give them to me. I told him he earned them—they were his alone, and we were all proud of him!

Both of my daughters were small and short. Seeing the size and height of the other swimmers on the starter blocks as they got into position, one would think that my girls did not have much of a chance of winning against the taller girls. When the gun went off and they hit the water, they were already a length ahead of my "short ones"!

To give Eileen and Jacque a fair chance, I made up for that height difference by continuously working with them to perfect their strokes, starts, and turns—and they became winners! But I have to stress: If you do not have a child who enjoys and just loves whatever sport they choose, no power on Earth is going to make them a winner. Neither of my girls would have stopped swimming, diving or gymnastics for anything!

When Jacque was nine years old, her elementary gym teacher, Mr. Franks, saw the potential of a gymnast in her and started coaching and entering her in gymnastics meets and, eventually, in the Colorado Women Open Gymnastic Meet held in Colorado Springs.

Jerry and I were out of town when we checked in with the girls to see how the meet turned out. Eileen was with Jacque at the meet. We were told by Jacque, "I didn't win anything."

I commented that one usually could not expect to win in a big meet like that, especially participating for the first time.

She just burst out laughing and said, "Ha, I won the silver medal!"

We could not believe it! As it turned out, the judges had to withhold her medal for a few hours because there was a protest lodged due to her age.

At that time, never before had a nine-year-old girl beaten seasoned, "older" gymnasts. Since no age limit had been posted, she was awarded the medal. The following year, the requirements and rules were changed. Jacque loved and was involved in gymnastics into her college years—not competitively, but just for fun.

Because of our love of skiing, Eileen had started skiing at the age of ten and Jacque, because of family circumstances, started at age three. Jacque fell in love with skiing and we could not stop her. I went on the rope tow with her and then she skied between my legs down the beginners' hill, repeating the process that I had started Eileen on.

After that, I took her on the ski lift in Vail, Colorado, up to midway. She looked down one of the steep hills and said, "I might have to fall" and off she went!

We had put her with both feet into one of the existing ski tracks because she could not ski with her feet apart. I went after her. When I passed two skiers standing at the side, looking down the ski slope, they called across the slope, asking me, "What was that just going by?"

I replied, "That was a little girl" and they just shook their heads.

As a teenager, Jacque skied every winter with her friend and her friend's father, both of whom were expert skiers. The father would never have accepted anything less than perfection from anyone skiing with him. Fortunately, Jacque was pretty fearless and tenacious, keeping up with them and becoming a fantastic skier, too. It was a pleasure to see the three of them floating down the slope, seemingly effortless in a graceful dance rhythm.

CHAPTER 16:

My "Citizen by Choice" Award

Although we loved skiing, swimming was still the big draw for my daughters and me. In addition to teaching regular and handicapped swimming classes, I also taught blind and blind/deaf students how to swim. My younger daughter, Jacqueline, was my "big" helper. She was a very small four years old at the time, but a big help. She would attend to my little students, be it either holding their hand while in the water or watching over them while they were sitting at the edge of the pool during the time I had some other student in the deep water. Or she would hold one little swimmer by the hand to jump with them off the diving board into deep water, where I was waiting to accept them. I would give my attention and the feeling of security to the little blind one having just jumped into the water, and lead them to the ladder. Jacqueline was self-sufficient and could swim to the ladder by herself and get out of the pool. It would have been much more difficult without her help and extra eyes.

My small class, including Jacque (who was in the middle of them, holding on to a kickboard—without it, you could not have even seen her), was featured in the Denver/Colorado *Recreation Magazine*.

I had very good results in my classes and, for my efforts, I was recognized by the City and County of Denver and the State of Colorado with the "American by Choice Distinguished Service Award," presented

91

to me at a surprise ceremony with all of the dignitaries of city, state and church in attendance.

The way I got to be nominated for that prestigious award was very funny and not very prestigious at all. At the time, I was vice president of the Littleton High School PTA. The president of the PTA, Mrs. Armstrong, was sitting in her bathroom on the potty when she heard the radio announcement that anyone knowing a naturalized citizen who did special community services should call a given number to nominate that person.

Well, there she was—the only paper available to her was toilet paper and she could only grab a lipstick to write the phone number down. Receiving that award was very humbling to me because I felt I really had not done anything special to deserve it. I had simply made many little souls happy to feel and be just like everybody else.

CHAPTER 17:

Helping out During the Vietnam War—Part One

During the Vietnam War, I quit teaching the swimming program for blind children and offered my services as a volunteer Red Cross nurse at Fitzsimmons Army Medical Center in Aurora, Colorado. This was the hospital where President Eisenhower had been treated when he needed medical attention for a heart attack. I volunteered to work there as a nurse in any capacity and on any station where help was needed the most. I ended up working on the amputee ward and in the cast room.

I recall when I had the opportunity to devote special time to attending a gravely injured young lieutenant who had to lie flat on his stomach because his whole backside was one big wound and he could not tolerate any covers. Being an officer, he was entitled to a private room, but he was so depressed and feeling so poorly that the doctors felt he would be better off and make better progress healing in a ward with others around him.

One of his doctors approached me and asked if I could give him some special attention. He was a tall, handsome, young man and did not have much of an appetite in his trying circumstances. He did not eat enough to promote his healing. I sat on the floor next to his special bed with an opening toward the floor for his face for him to see and to be fed, looking up and talking to him. I fed him and encouraged him to eat talk and maybe read a little. I even left the hospital in search of special foods (particularly ice cream) to tempt his appetite. My efforts seemed to lift his spirits and he looked forward to my coming to see him. I believe my extra care and attention helped him heal a little faster. After a time, he got well enough to be moved to his own room. I continued to visit him.

In addition to nursing, I also spent time helping to rehabilitate amputees. I worked with the amputees in the pools at Fitzsimmons Army Medical Center and at Lowry Air Force Base in Denver. I helped them adjust their balance and get used to the loss of limbs. It gave me a good feeling to assist the instructors who were teaching the amputees scuba-diving, providing them with supervised recreation and boosting their bruised confidence. It was a gratifying experience.

The amputees were always better scuba-diving students than the uninjured ones, and enjoyed proving to themselves and others that they could still do what everyone else was able to do. They were a pleasure to work with.

I was asked by an orthopedic surgeon, who had amputated several limbs from a young man, if I could help the patient get used to his loss of limbs by working in the pool. I was happy to do so and, as it turned out, he was a big, tall Native American who had lost the lower part of his left leg and most of his right arm above the elbow.

The doctor warned me that his patient would most likely not crack a smile or talk to me more than a few grunts. He asked me not to get discouraged and felt that this young man needed my help more than the others.

My Native American patient was hard to handle just because of his large size. He also did not know how to swim. For this strong young man, just having been in the water was a new element, and having only the use of one leg and one arm had to make him feel pretty helpless. On top of it all, he was being entrusted into the hands of a petite, five-foot-tall female swimming instructor!

Both of us learned together how to deal with his buoyancy in the water. Each session became easier and more fun. We laughed and giggled. In fact, we both could have drowned in three feet of water for being so silly! Since he did not know how to swim, I took the opportunity to teach him swimming, using his handicap to his advantage. It was easier for me that he did not know how to swim because he did not have to "unlearn" any habits. I successfully "water-proofed" my big friend, and he was so proud of himself for having learned how to swim, which was a positive accomplishment. Unlike the doctor's prediction, he talked with me a lot, and I still remember him fondly.

Another happy memory involves a one-legged Marine SEAL, who could "out-swim" and "outdo" anyone. He taught my daughter, Eileen, how to scuba dive. When her husband had left for a tour of duty in Vietnam, she felt so lost at first that she asked me for help. It was a natural fit for her to get involved in my Red Cross activities.

She received lessons from my Marine SEAL friend, became an excellent scuba diver, and continued working with the recuperating vets and amputees. She enjoyed scuba diving so much that she took the opportunity to dive in the open waters of Hawaii a day ahead of her husband's coming there for R and R (Rest and Recreation) from Vietnam.

When I volunteered to do nursing at Fitzsimmons during the Vietnam War, I assumed that there were more swimming instructors available than nurses. I quit the program teaching swimming to my little blind and blind and deaf students, hoping there were others to take my place.

Unfortunately, that was not the case; even though there were plenty of instructors, none came forward to take over that particular program. I had started the program and the classes seven years prior, and was disappointed that it was discontinued, but I was also committed to helping at Fitzsimmons Medical Center. As far as I know, I was the only one who ever created and ran a program like that single-handedly.

The school for the blind would send my students by school bus to the Curtis Street Public Swimming Pool in Denver, where I would be waiting for them. Their parents would pick them up at the end of each class. I just loved these children and missed seeing them.

It saddened me and brought back a saying my German mother used a lot because I was always trying to do everything and be everywhere at practically the same time. "Inge," she said, "you cannot dance at two weddings at the same time with one 'popo'" (meaning "tush"). I know that is true, but I am still trying to beat the odds.

CHAPTER 18:

Helping out During the Vietnam War—Part Two

In May and April 1957, the Vietnam Baby Lift was brought to life and became extremely active, delivering many orphaned babies to be adopted in America, Canada, and Europe. The babies arrived in Denver, one of the stop-over cities, mostly at night on their way to different destinations. Some of the hopeful parents-to-be flew from all over the world to these different delivery points to pick up one of these little babies to become part of their family.

I was one of the volunteers needed in Denver at the Lowery Air Force Base to attend to these little souls, most of whom were in very poor shape. These babies were bodies with dangling limbs. They spent their short existence almost untouched, being fed, diapered and put back into their make-shift beds. They had not been cuddled or cradled, and received no stimulation whatsoever.

Almost all had severe diarrhea and projectile vomiting. Volunteer doctors were on call day and night to attend to them. However, they did not have enough time with the babies to properly assess and address their physical needs. The efforts and the goal for all of us were to keep the little souls alive and as comfortable as possible. I remember a young doctor holding a baby and saying, "Only God knows how far this baby can be rehabilitated," pointing out the total lack of strength in the little arms and legs.

Annually, the Vietnam babies who survived get together and celebrate. However, like most volunteers who do their jobs and move on, the dozens of men and woman who donated their time in this extremely urgent, emergency situation—some working nights and going back to work on their regular jobs during the day—do not get together or even get mentioned for their efforts.

First of all, it would be impossible because so many were involved in so many different ways at so many different times. However, I remember those volunteers and their acts of kindness every time I read about the Vietnam babies getting together. Those volunteers saw what they needed to do and did it the best they could. The babies' attempts to get used to food caused problems with projectile vomiting and diarrhea that made it necessary for us volunteers to take off all of our clothes in the shower with us, before actually taking a shower, to rid ourselves of the vomit, urine, and feces.

The only things we volunteers would have liked to know (even today) are how many babies survived the airlifts and if there was anything more we could have done to increase those numbers. We like to think that the majority made it to the waiting parents, who took over the tasks that were so freely and lovingly given by the volunteers.

Many acts of kindness were performed in April and May of 1975, in the successful Vietnam Baby Airlift program. Bless the volunteers who helped make miracles happen!

Acts of Kindness in the Vietnam Baby Airlift

The Vietnam Baby Airlift gave new meaning to "Acts of Kindness." The entire project required abundant planning and work by many volunteers. It started with air crews including attendants, nurses and doctors loading babies in military aircraft in Vietnam and unloading them, in our case at Denver, Colorado. More volunteer attendants, nurses and doctors took over. Few of the babies, mostly from overcrowded orphanages were well. Their bodies had no muscle tone. Those babies that survived have grown-up and have reunions in Denver. Much attention is given to them in the newspapers, radio and T.V. during their reunions. They are happy to be alive and functioning as well they should be. None of this would have been possible, of course without the many thousand Acts of Kindness and of course the U.S. taxpayer

CHAPTER 19:

*Teaching Water Safety and Life Saving to
Handicapped Children and Others*

Although Jerry and I had built a beautiful home with a swimming pool
in Littleton, there were not many private pools in the Denver area at
that time. Some of our neighbors kept horses for their children and
my daughters were invited to ride them and had fun doing so. Their
children had an open invitation to come and swim in our pool at designated times. We had worked out a system where I rang a big bell to
let them know they could come over.

I was no longer giving handicapped swimming lessons, but I was
getting quite a reputation as a swimming teacher. I taught babies as
young as three months old. They would "swim" above me, looking
down at me, doing the natural dog paddle, and following me while I
swam on my back under them. I was, of course, in very close contact
with them. When the toddlers came for their lessons, I only had to be
in the pool, stretching my arms out to them, and they would toddle
right into the pool, reaching out for me, then fall into my arms and we
would go under water together.

I "water-proofed" quite a few toddlers whose parents were being transferred and moving to warmer climates and into houses with
swimming pools. They were afraid to have a small child around a pool.
One of the favorite, fun Red Cross classes I taught was to expectant

parents. I called it "How to Teach Your Unborn Child to Swim." I remember one expectant father asking me "How are you going to do that?" Later I taught some of the parents of that same group to help their toddlers how to swim.

I had a lot of fun teaching high school students Water Safety and Life Saving classes because most of my students, especially the boys, were taller than me. We giggled a lot when I had to teach them how to float. Boys are physically built so much different than girls. They tend to "sink" from the hips down. So they had to learn to become at ease while floating with just their head tilted back and face up, arms stretched out to the side, and feet floating down, putting them in a "standing position." I kept telling them to pretend they were standing outside the pool, face up to the sun, with their arms stretched out, so they would look like they were shouting, "Oh, this feels good!"

What made teaching them to float even more fun was that the boys over six feet tall had to bend their knees so that the ones near the shallow end of our pool would not touch the bottom of the pool with their feet.

Swimming and the water was a big part of our lives. The girls and I were forever in the water, under water, at swimming and diving meets, or teaching swimming. At one early swimming meet at the Columbine Country Club in Colorado, where Eileen was competing, the starter gun went off and she dove into the pool. Her little sister, Jacqueline, jumped at the same time into the nearby baby pool and "raced" across it. That was the beginning of Jacque's swimming career.

We had fun; our summers were busy and filled with swimming and swimming-related events, and the girls enjoyed being with their teammates and learned a lot from each other.

Eileen belonged to the Denver University Hill Toppers Swim Team at the age of eleven. She competed in swimming events and was also a competitive diver for the team. She did well in all of her different strokes but excelled in the breast stroke. Jacque joined that same team at the age of four-and-a-half and competed as well, also excelling in the breast stroke. In Germany, the breast stroke was very popular, and

I grew up swimming that stroke for miles in the Hafel River. I continued swimming the breast stroke all of my life.

One summer, I was coerced into coaching the swim team at a private riding club where we were members. Previous arrangements for a coach fell through and the club was in a bind. I was told that my background made me a logical choice. Reluctantly, I agreed to coach that summer, but it turned out well and we all had fun.

During the summers, I attended swimming meets regularly as a Red Cross Water Safety Instructor, officiating in different capacities as a judge, a timer, or whatever was needed. One time at the AAU (American Amateur Union) meet, I was officiating as a stroke judge and had to disqualify my daughter Eileen, who was winning at that point, because of a wrong foot position on a turn. She understood and it was no big deal to her.

Another time I was a judge in charge of watching the "touch" and "turns." I had to watch Jacque, who had swallowed a "muggy" from the backwash at the end of the pool and hung on, coughing to clear her lungs. As I was bending over to check her turn, I had to disqualify her. She gasped, "I know, Mom, I know I'm disqualified." She then turned and finished the race.

My life was fun and crazy at the same time. Parents begged me to teach their children how to swim. There were few private swimming teachers available and none with the use of their own pool, except me. I am sure that enhanced my popularity as a swimming teacher.

It was fun when young people approached me later on and reminded me who they were and that I taught them how to swim. I even got to teach some of *their* children. Both Eileen and Jacque naturally learned how to teach swimming by assisting me. They became Water Safety Instructors themselves and continued teaching.

CHAPTER 20:

Eating Salad Without Dressing and the
German Word for "Shower"

We thought everybody knew men cannot take a dusche, except maybe foreigners—but I'm getting ahead of my story. A shower is spelled "dusche" in Germany. Believe me, my heart went out to those unaware of that. I had my share of faux pas, too, when I first came to the United States.

Littleton's tiny shopping area had a beautiful children's clothing store that we frequented for my girls and me. Being little and small, I had trouble buying adult sizes. That was the time before they finally made "petite" sizes, so I bought nice, simple dresses there.

The owner's husband worked for Otis Elevator Company and she called me to ask a favor. Her husband, who was the Otis Elevator regional manager, had gotten notice by the IIE (International Institute of Education) that three well-known, prominent German architects were scheduled to come to Denver to look at the one and only existing "walking walkway" in Denver. Today, every airport has such walkways and we think nothing of it. But this was in 1959.

I was glad to help out, although no one knew what the expected guests looked like or even how old they might be. We agreed that I'd go to the airport with the Otis representative and try to pick German-looking men out of the crowd. If they had spoken English and communicated well, I should have felt free to leave them in the care of the Otis agent.

I approached three men whom I thought might be German and addressed them in German. They all rushed me and gave me warm hugs. The traditional German make-up is usually most reserved, but their actions were not reserved. They exclaimed how happy they were that someone finally spoke German. They had been in California for two weeks looking at buildings and having difficulties with translations, etc.

Because of the language barrier, I agreed to accompany the host and his three guests to dinner at the country club. When we agreed upon a time to pick them up at the hotel, they happily exclaimed, "Good, we'll have enough time to take a 'dusche!'" Their plans were to take a shower.

I inquired delicately how much longer they planned to stay in the United States and they replied, "A few more weeks, visiting New York and Philadelphia." I thought it best to explain that only women could take 'dusches' in America and everyone else takes 'showers.' They were terribly embarrassed but were grateful that they did not have to make the same mistake again.

Later, when I translated the menu at dinner, I asked them which kind of the various dressings listed they would like.

"Dressings? What is that?" they asked.

When I explained, they told me they had been serving themselves from the buffet tables and did not see any dressings. They thought it was a strange custom in the United States.

It pleased me to make their eating experience more pleasant for the rest of their stay. A simple act of kindness, again, for which they were most grateful.

CHAPTER 21:

Helping to Reinforce International Education

We also entertained dignitaries from foreign countries for the Institute of International Education IIE which brought them into American homes to meet families and generally learn about American life. Doing this, we made good friends. One especially was Eduard Adorno, minister of Baden Wuertenberg. His estate was located on a low mountain overlooking the Bodensee (Lake Constance) at the border of Switzerland. Minister Adorno was the right hand of President Adenauer of Germany for many years.

Since I was supervising our construction jobs, we as a family had to work around that part to make room to entertain foreign visitors. The way we met him was through the IIE and agreeing to host him for a German dinner at our house and had agreed to pick him up at his hotel.

The way I usually managed these occasional visits was by setting the table the night before, cooking ahead the day before, and putting the food into a timed oven. Because of conflict with dates that just could not be changed, I had to supervise pouring concrete at our construction site for an eighteen-unit apartment house on the same day (all day) as his visit. I was young and energetic, so it never slowed me down.

I just picked Mr. Adorno up at his hotel on the way home. Dinner was ready to be served when we got there and we sat down to eat. Our teenage daughter, Eileen, saw to it that her little sister, Jacqueline (seven years younger), behaved and everything was under control. She was always responsible and a big help to me.

Only after the meal did I realize that I had forgotten to change out of the clothing that I had worn while pouring concrete. But what are a few flecks of concrete on pants? Like I had mentioned before, I always looked presentable, even on a construction site! I did remember to wash my hands, and the meal turned out great. And a great friendship started at that evening. We visited each other's homes often and were good friends with Mr. Eduard Adorno and his wife, Heidi, until he died.

CHAPTER 22:

Throwing Plums at a German Bishop

In 1971 we were asked by the IIE (International Institute of Education) in Denver to host the Lutheran "Bischof" (Bishop) Lilje of Hanover, Germany, as a guest of the U.S. government.

We were delighted to do so and agreed to have him for dinner at our house. I invited Dr. Noren, the pastor of our Swedish Lutheran church, and his wife to help us host the distinguished guest and they were honored to do so.

When foreign visitors were away from their home for any length of time, I always made it a point to serve them a meal "from home" using recipes from their respective countries. That attempt was quite challenging at times but very much appreciated by the guests.

Since Bischof Lilje came from Germany, I cooked a German dinner. He was delighted and enjoyed every bite. I even baked a German Pflaumen Kuchen (plum cake) for him since these Italian special plums were just in season. As it turned out, he was a diabetic and could not eat it.

It looked so beautiful that I at least wanted to show it to him before cutting it. As I entered the dining room, carrying the coffee pot and the cake with my left hand, I hit the doorjamb and it fell out of my hands face-down onto the white carpet.

I just stood there and laughed. My teenage daughter, Jacqueline, came to my aid. She turned up her eyes at me then looked down at the purple, juicy mess on that white carpet and said, "Mom, that is not funny!" I personally thought it was one of the funnier things I did—and it was an accident.

Dr. Noren jumped up, flipped the cake over and back onto the baking sheet, and said, pointing at one of the blobs on the carpet, "I want that piece!" We all laughed and I proceeded to serve the dessert and everyone ate it with special glee! It was, after all, a very successful dinner party.

When all had quieted down, Bischof Lilje said, "When I get home, I will report to my congregations in Germany that the Americans did not only throw themselves at my feet, but also their Pflaumen Kuchen!"

Because of his anti-Hitler and anti-war opinions, Bishop Lilje had been very much pursued by the Nazi party and their anti-Christian propaganda. His life was constantly endangered. Finally, the Nazis arrested, incarcerated, and sentenced him to death.

The advancing American troops liberated Bischof Lilje from death row one hour before he was to be executed by the Nazis! He told us his religious and political opinions were such that he had been declared an enemy of the "German Volk."

His fate at the time was not unusual and many innocent, ordinary people (as well as famous ones) could not be saved. They were not reached in time by the American troops and died horrible deaths in the last hours of the terrible war.

CHAPTER 23:

Daughter Eileen Marrying the Love of her Life at the Air Force Academy in Colorado Springs, Colorado

We had moved to Littleton, Colorado, in 1956, and both Eileen and Jacque went through the Littleton school system and graduated from Littleton High School with a solid foundation for their college education.

Eileen was student body president in her senior year at Littleton High. She graduated with advanced standing credits and went on to the University of Colorado in Boulder, graduating in three years as a Phi Betta Kappa. She always had good study habits and combined those habits with a quest for perfection.

Through an invitation to a tea dance sponsored by Littleton High School and the Air Force Academy in Colorado Springs, some sixty miles south of Littleton, she was introduced to Richard Engel, a cadet from Tulsa, Oklahoma, in his first year at the academy. They became good friends and their relationship grew through her remaining high school years. Dick escorted her to her junior and senior proms. That friendship blossomed into love.

She graduated on Monday, June 4, 1968. Dick graduated as a second lieutenant on Wednesday, June 6, and they got married on Saturday,

June 9, in the beautiful Air Force Academy Chapel in Colorado Springs. The reception followed at the officers' club.

An Air Force Academy Chapel Wedding June 9, 1968

Dick came back to the academy for a tour as a flight instructor. During that tour, their son, Chad, was born at the Air Force Academy. Chad became a firefighter and paramedic at the Henderson, Nevada, Fire Department.

Daughter Kristin was also born at the Air Force Academy. After graduation from college in Las Vegas, she became a 911 operator for several years. It was an emotionally draining job, so she decided to switch careers and become a kindergarten teacher.

For a long time during her teen years, Eileen was involved in swimming and diving, and she collected many blue ribbons. I remember that at one meet she was swimming the breast stroke and was idling along because she was used to winning. When I saw a newcomer catching up with her, I yelled, "EILEEN!" It was spontaneous on my part, but she heard me, sped up, and won. When she climbed out of the pool, she came to me and asked, "Mom, what happened?" I told her about the new challenger. She said she thought something was up when I yelled her name. We had many such funny "happenings."

Eileen and Dick are now the proud grandparents of a beautiful boy named Brody, who made me a great-grandmother. Brody turned four years old in July 2009.

After graduation, Dick completed flight training and served as a forward air controller for two years in Vietnam. While he was flying, Eileen stayed with us. The negative political attitude her father displayed upset her so she decided to move in with a friend whose husband was also flying in Vietnam.

To counteract her father's negativity, and to support the military in Vietnam, Eileen founded "Colorado Cares for the POWs and MIAs." She held a big Fourth of July rally at the capitol building in downtown Denver that attracted hundreds of people from the Denver area. Many Vietnam War veterans, active military personnel and their families attended. Of course, it also attracted a lot of war protestors.

Eileen was prepared to deal with the protestors. A very pretty petite, cute, four-foot-eleven-inch blonde, she had to interrupt the principal speaker when the protestors got to be too loud. Being so little, she had to stand on a box to be able to look over the speaker's podium to plead with the reporters and cameramen, "Please do not give them the attention they so rudely demand."

Hats and newspapers were immediately used by attendees to cover cameras pointed in the directions of the protestors. The rally was a huge success and Eileen made national news. Dick read about her efforts in the *Stars and Stripes* military newspaper while in Vietnam.

After retiring as a lieutenant-colonel from the Air Force, Dick became a pilot for Continental Airlines and is now retired. Eileen and Dick live in Henderson, Nevada. Eileen is now a successful real estate agent there.

In the past Eileen taught school for many years. Their son Chad is a fire fighter and paramedic and their daughter Krissy is a Kindergarden teacher. Chad's wife, Vanessa is from San Diego. They have a new son Brody. Dick is now enjoying his beautiful home and pool, which he was not able to do much of while working for Continental and flying out of Newark, N J.

I am proud of my daughters and the lives they have created for themselves. I hope that they have benefited in a small way from learning some of the childhood experiences that I shared with them as they grew up.

CHAPTER 24:

*My First One-Hundred-Foot Scuba
Dive off the Coast of Jamaica*

I traveled and cruised extensively all throughout my married life, and in any city or island I visited, I made arrangements to dive and hire a diver if possible, to accompany me. Having been a serious diver, I traveled with my own equipment and wet suit. I did not check the diving bag on the plane for fear it might get lost or delayed. I could do without my other bags, but I would have been heartbroken had my diving gear been lost. My short, petite stature made it difficult to rent properly fitting equipment, and children's gear did not fit me either since the kids were bigger than I was.

In Jamaica, I hired two divers, one to be my guide and the other to stand by waiting in the boat, in case of an emergency. We had a fabulous dive with practically unlimited visibility. On the way down, we passed a few large traps filled with various types of fish, and I stopped at each one to study them.

The diver kept urging me on by tapping the diving watch to remind me that we had limited time. When reaching the one-hundred-foot mark, and lingering briefly at that depth, I had accomplished my goal. My guide and I checked and compared our air supplies. Fortunately, I had no problems staying down an hour on one tank. Most of the time,

I had the same slow breathing pattern as the guides and we did not have to adjust the air supply or shorten my diving time.

My guide and I were ascending from our hundred-foot dive, swimming gradually at an upward angle toward our waiting diver and boat (one takes this precaution to not ascend too quickly in order to prevent getting the "bends"). He was swimming just about ten feet ahead of me, rotating constantly to keep vigil against any unwanted surprises.

We swam along happily and the guide had just turned and looked at me to ask if I was okay, and I had given him the okay sign, forming a circle with my index finger and thumb, so he kept turning. Then, out of nowhere, close to my right side, I could have touched the biggest fish I had ever seen this close to me on any dive. I took the diving knife fastened on my right calf and banged on my tank to attract my guide's attention, since the water carries and magnifies any sound.

He turned immediately, saw the fish, readied his harpoon, and chased after him. In that beautiful, deep blue water, fish appear suddenly out of nowhere and disappear just as fast.

The guide later estimated it to have been at least fifteen feet long. It was a bluish color and beautiful! When we reached the waiting boat's ladder, I quickly took my mouthpiece out, pushed my mask up, and asked, "Was that a tuna fish?" Both men laughed heartily and, to my surprise, my guide replied that it had been a barracuda!

I had seen many barracuda before but they were a light beige color with black, spotted markings. None had been longer than three feet, and I had encountered most of them in five to ten feet of water while searching for shells.

When I got home, I went to the library (there was no Internet at that time) and researched barracudas. Sure enough, there was a picture of "my" big, fifteen-foot long fish. It looked the same and had the same bluish-gray color.

I found that the deeper one dives, the bigger the fish seem to be. I also noticed the species of fish changing practically foot by foot as you descend.

I was seventy-five years old when I dove on the Australian barrier reef with a small group of twenty-something-year-olds. I was shorter than they were by at least a foot and had much smaller feet than my companions, especially when wearing fins. It put me at quite a disadvantage speed-wise! But they put up with me, and I with them.

I had the good fortune to dive practically everywhere diving is good! In the Bahamas, Jamaica, Puerto Rico, Cozumel, Tortola, the Virgin Islands, Caracas, Venezuela, on the Australia barrier reef, and the beautiful reefs in Belize, British Honduras.

Unfortunately, I had an accident eight years ago, severely injuring both of my shoulders, which restricted my physical activities and especially hindered my swimming. One of the big plant storage containers, which was fully loaded and on rollers without brakes, rolled down an incline at a Lowe's store in Aurora, Colorado, and hit my right foot from the back, almost severing the Achilles heel tendon. I was thrown forward at full-length, ending up with my face in a flat of pansies I was carrying. Rotator cuffs were torn in both shoulders, and I was bloodied all over—looking spectacular!

I am still in constant pain and limited in my movements to this date. I do miss my swimming terribly! But I am still in constant motion, doing something or another on a daily basis. At least there is always walking!

CHAPTER 25:

*I Started Something New for the
Caribbean Cruise Ships*

When I became district sales manager for NCL (Norwegian Caribbean Cruise Lines) for Colorado, Wyoming, and Montana, I was embarking on another "unbelievable adventure." The job was offered and given to me in a funny way since I had never applied for it.

We had been their customers, had traveled on their beautiful ships frequently, and enjoyed the cruises. Our bookings out of Denver, however, were totally unsatisfactory and repeatedly caused us great inconvenience. We were booked into hotels in Fort Lauderdale, some thirty miles away from Miami, near the pier where the Norwegian Cruise Line vessels docked and boarded.

In the 1950s and '60s, the cruise industry was just beginning to come of age. At that time, travel agents in Denver and all of Colorado were not familiar with the industry and had not received any training by the various cruise companies.

Finally, I wrote to NCL and told them that just because we lived in Colorado did not mean we did not like to cruise! Would they please train the Colorado travel agents so we could get better and more knowledgeable service?

The next thing I knew, one of their district managers flew from Chicago to Denver to interview me and immediately offered me the job to educate the travel industry in three states; Colorado, Wyoming, and Montana. I was going through a divorce at the time and was delighted to take the job.

Eventually, I was responsible for having the cruise line create an air-sea package out of Denver with Braniff Airlines. With the help of Braniff's sales representatives, it was fun to organize big cruise presentations in my three states.

I had been an avid scuba-diver since 1965, and had been diving in all the ports their ships visited. I suggested and stressed the fact that they should use the very thing they were trying to sell, the beautiful blue waters of the Caribbean. Why not offer scuba-diving and snorkeling packages? My suggestion was implemented and became one of their biggest attractions and best-selling programs offered.

I had never worked for a big corporation before and even though I liked NCL's principal owners, my instincts told me to keep my own insurance and stay independent with one foot out the door all throughout my employment there. I took the job only for fun and travel because it helped me get back into the world of being single after the divorce. I was financially secure and looked forward to fulfilling some of my dreams.

Even though I worked out of Colorado, away from the corporate office in Miami, I did not like working in a big corporation. The more I observed how people were treated, the more I disliked and distrusted that environment even more.

My parents, grandparents, former husband, and I were self-employed and I valued that independence and guarded it. When two vice presidents, my friends in that corporation, were treated dishonestly and pushed out of their jobs by the very district manager who interviewed me, I quit!

At that time, I never analyzed the reasons for all of the events, but I knew I did not want any part of it. Writing this now and looking back at that president—a young, ambitious man who made himself successful by promoting *my* ideas and using the beautiful waters of the Caribbean for diving and snorkeling packages, as well as offering picnics on the beaches of small islands—I'm sure he caused the two vice presidents, both good men, to lose their well-earned jobs, and I was impressed that my instincts had served me well.

As time passed, he became president of another small cruise line, but the harm he had done previously was long-reaching and caught up with him. Not long after that, the newspapers reported that the cruise line he was president of had suffered from scandals and all kinds of other moral problems, and he had been let go.

When I worked for NCL, I met many Norwegian officers of the Royal Caribbean Cruise Line. They all loved to dive and I was often invited along on their diving and snorkeling opportunities. A group of the officers would hire a dive boat and dive guides in the various ports and graciously invite me to go with them.

I was offered the use of their personal diving equipment even when they were on duty and could not dive with me. After the dive, I was encouraged to bring back the "dirty" diving gear and dump it in their shower, having been assured that it was really no problem for them to clean it! They asked me, "What are friends for?" Friends they were, and were welcomed by me in Denver whenever they wanted to visit.

One time, while five of us were diving off Cozumel, Mexico, my companions were out of air and were back in the guide boat enjoying a beer after we had a fruitful dive, bringing up various kinds of fish. Diving around Cozumel is different from many other areas because of the extremely swift currents there.

(One of the NCL ships once had to anchor out because of the strong winds in Cozumel, and the captain's boat had to take a patient ashore to be flown to the mainland. The winds and waves were strong and the swift current caused the cruise ship to run over its own anchor chain, breaking it. The ship had to cruise back and forth, waiting for the boat to return to the ship so it could be hoisted back into its cradle.)

Sport-divers had to take extreme precaution not to lose sight of the dive boat above. It followed their air bubbles and the towed diving flag along the surface, indicating that there were divers below. If careless, an emerging diver might have to swim miles on the surface to find the boat to get back to shore. It could be a pretty strenuous swim, depending on the size of the waves and the strength of the current at that time.

One of the diving guides and I were still down when he checked my remaining air supply and compared it with his pressure gauge. He gave me the okay sign, indicating that we still had a good amount of air available. He tucked my arm into his and off we went, looking for lobsters. I could dive about an hour on one tank of air; my husband, Jim, and most other men usually used up a tank in twenty minutes and had to surface to get to the dive boat to exchange bottles or quit diving.

It was an adventure in itself to learn how and where to look for lobsters. As I recall, we found five or six good-size lobsters by the time we were running low on air and had to get back to the boat. It was fun to share them with everyone at a camp fire later.

To this day, I feel that if one loves the water and is a good swimmer, it would be such a fabulous adventure to learn what is to be seen in the ocean. You have not lived your life fully if you have not seen the wonders waiting for you below the surface!

CHAPTER 26:

Modeling the First "Wheeled Luggage" in the World
for the Samsonite Corporation

Life is funny! In so many ways, it plays tricks on people. For instance, when you tell someone that your friend is a model, what do you picture her to look like? Most likely you think of a tall, beautiful young lady walking down a runway, or posing for pictures in magazines. But I bet it is not the picture of a five-foot-tall, fifty-two-year-old woman, right?

Well, there's the trick! I was the oldest of three selected models when I took my last professional modeling job in 1977 for the Samsonite Corporation, makers of luggage in Denver, Colorado.

It was days before I was getting married. My future husband, Jim Johnston, had the unique opportunity to watch his future wife make history by modeling and presenting to the world the first suitcases on wheels! All posters and marketing material proclaimed: "Samsonite Freewheelin' Travelers."

The Samsonite Corporation had rejected two prior "shoots", which was not good for that crew and was also expensive. It took about sixteen people with different specialties to put a shoot together ranging from a director down. I was one of four women interviewed for the job. There were to be three models in the photograph. I was selected to be the third person. Because I was small and older, not really fitting into their previous picture and advertising attempts, they decided to take a totally different approach with me when doing this third shoot.

When I was hired, they kept stressing that I was "the" main person, etc. My reply to all that talk was, "Oh, yeah, I bet!"

Having fun being the "Senior Model" for the wheeled luggage.

So I was surprised when I realized that it really was true and that everything depended on my being accepted by Samsonite. They used my overall appearance and the presence I projected: My hair was pinned up into a French twist, sprayed gray, and I had to wear one of my own dresses since the wardrobe they had brought was too big for me. I selected a black dress with a short jacket, embellished with a light gray ascot and a white mink boa around my neck and carried white gloves in my free hand to complement the white of my roller skates.

So there we were, three models: a beautiful, young lady posing in the back on one side , a nice-looking young man posing in front of her but on the other side, and me in front of them. Each of us was pulling or pushing a wheeled Samsonite suitcase. I was pushing mine. The cameras were focusing on me, the prominent model.

The shoot took place outside, on an elevated bank entrance on marble steps at the Cherry Creek Shopping Center Mall in Denver. Sounds simple, doesn't it? Not so! Would you believe we were on roller skates on a marble surface, pushing the suitcases ahead of us? That was not so bad for the other two, who knew how to roller-skate; also, only one of their skates were showing in the ad, so they could stand on the other foot which was with out the roller skate.

That was not the case for me. Both of my roller skates had to be seen. I had never roller-skated and had no idea how to do it. I was supposed to stand on one skate with the other skate up in the air behind me, like I was really sailing along—and I was supposed to do that during the whole day's shoot.

Each of us had a personal coach assigned who was responsible to watch our positions, facial expressions, smiles, hands positioned on the handles of the suitcases, etc. My coach asked me if I could lift my leg even briefly to make it look like I was really skating. I told them to shoot fast since I could not guarantee how long I would remain standing. However, I was able to hold the pose several times and the shoot turned out well, without my falling on my butt.

I do not know how many of you are aware that the cameras they use for these shoots are extremely sensitive. The marble surface we were standing on was continually swept to keep it clean of footprints and sand. They used artificial light with various umbrellas over them to enforce the daylight, even on a clear day. It is quite an effort to get good pictures.

The reason I mention all this is that they could not tape or in any way block my skate's ball bearings from moving since anything like that would have been visible. I just had to grin and bear it! I think I had my toes curled right through my shoes and skates into the marble to stay upright.

The producer and crew were pleased at day's end with the finished product. They called me as soon as they were notified to let me know that the Samsonite Corporation had accepted me as the model and the whole new shoot. All was well!

After learning I was about to get married, the management of the Samsonite Corporation sent two sets of the new-model suitcases with rollers as a wedding gift to me. I thought that was extremely nice.

The photos that were taken and accepted by Samsonite were on all the marketing materials used in that promotion around the world. Among them were big posters and point-of-sale folders. They offered to give me several posters, which I proudly accepted as a memento of my last modeling job before setting off on my new, married-life adventure.

Modeling St. John's Women's Apparel. I am the short one.

CHAPTER 27:

My "Laser," the Smallest U.S. Olympic-Class Racing Sailboat

I knew that the Norwegian tennis pro who had been giving me lessons had a sailboat. When I questioned him and explained that I was interested in buying one, he suggested the "Laser," the smallest Olympic-class sailboat the United States had. He thought that the Laser would suit my temperament since he knew I would want a boat I could handle by myself.

The Laser was just what I was looking for. I could sail it by myself but two could sail it, if need be. I wanted to be independent and able to go sailing any time without having to ask someone else to help me handle the boat.

Great! I went to the Marina located on Parker Road and Holly Street in Denver to look at one. After I spoke with the owner, I was shown a model of the Laser. I took one look and fell in love with it.

As it so happened, a big two-day Laser workshop was scheduled beginning the next day, a Saturday, at the Cherry Creek Reservoir in Denver. A visiting champion team of the Laser fleet from San Francisco Bay, California, was in Denver to conduct it. I was invited as the guest of the marina owner to attend the first day of the workshop in the command boat and observe to see if I would like the performance of the Laser. I was happy to accept! I was excited and could hardly wait until the next day.

The next morning, bright and early on what promised to be a beautiful day, I was the first one at the reservoir, eagerly waiting for them. As the demonstrations and instructions proceeded, I knew I had found my dream boat! I told them I wanted to buy a Laser. "What color?" they asked me, and I replied, "Any color, as long as you can bring it to the reservoir the next day."

Sunday morning, I accepted my little blue Laser with glee! It was put into the water for me; all I had to do was get in it and off I went, following the instructions like I knew how to sail. I did not capsize and even beached it without an incident! I was sure I was in heaven. Where else could I have sailed my own Laser?

At the time, I drove a red 1975 Mustang, and got a trailer hitch put on to pull my Laser. I went sailing at the reservoir every day. I could handle my trailer with my Laser just fine. I could launch my boat without any trouble then walk it to a nice spot on the beach and go back and park my Mustang. The sail had to be sleeved onto the mast of the Laser but with all of my five feet, I could not step the mast into place. I had to make it work for me, so I laid the mast down, sleeved the sail on it, laid the boat on its side, stuck the mast sideways into the provided place, righted the boat again, pushed it into the water, and off I went. To take the mast down, I just reversed the procedure. No big deal. The sailors around me thought that was a wonderful invention and told me I should have it patented.

Well, what a rude awakening on my first few solo attempts to sail my Laser. Here I was, a fifty-two-year-old woman who had never sailed before, with no one there to give me instructions from a command boat, and the winds blowing ideally but I capsized over and over. I had no trouble righting my boat but I did not know how to keep it up.

I was such a beginner, not having any idea what to do to sail a boat and not knowing that I had to turn the boat into the wind to reduce the wind resistance of the sail in order to right the boat and keep it up that way. I was in the water for the umpteenth time, hanging on to the dagger board and catching my breath, contemplating how and what to do, when the park rangers came by in their motorboat.

Looking down at me, they said, "Ma'am, do you know how to right your boat?"

I replied, "Perfectly! But I do not know how to keep it up."

They were polite and did not laugh out loud! I accepted their offer to pull me in, and told them I appreciated their help since I was a bit tired but had a date to play a game of tennis that evening, which I just could not miss.

As it turned out, I had a fantastic game! I had gotten rid of my usual excess energy playing with my boat in and out of the water, so I could control my ball well.

I also had no trouble handling my Laser in the back of my Mustang. I could even park my Mustang as well as my boat in the underground garage of my apartment house. I had so much fun and was so happy to have my boat; it seemed I did not even touch the ground walking!

After having sailed daily my first week, I had no more fingernails left from knotting the lines to fasten my mast on to the boat. I called the marina and told them, "Hey, fellows, there has to be a better way to fasten the mast on to the boat than just tying it on. My fingernails are gone and my hands are sore!"

"Come to the marina and we'll get you a 'ratchet,'" I was told.

I drove to the marina, pulling my Laser, and when I walked in, my buddies, the San Francisco Laser champions, were still in Denver at the marina. When they saw me, they all hollered, "Hey, Inge!"

At that, everybody in that showroom looked up at me standing there on the steps. I was such a hit with them, being an older woman who was learning how to sail a Laser. On top of the boat being so demanding, I was also the only woman sailing it in the Colorado Laser fleet. They just loved it!

The owner of the marina had tried his best to discourage me from buying that boat. He told me it was fast, wet, and unforgiving. "You either sail or you swim. There is nothing in between!"

My answer was, "I taught swimming for twenty-five years for the Red Cross at all levels, and if I'll swim a lot before I sail, that's okay, as long as I become a hot shot sailor."

Well, I did swim a lot until I became a hot shot sailor! I even learned to "come about" by turning the boat into the wind, making it a gentler turn, after somebody told me I did not have to "jibe" all the time. Jibing is turning the boat to offer the wind the broad side of the sail and the side of the boat, making it a fast and violent turn. Unwittingly, I had practiced the harder turn to perfection. Oh, ignorance was bliss for me. Whatever it took! As long as I was sailing, it was okay with me.

As I was walking down the stairs in the marina, my future husband (I did not know it at the time) was standing at the bottom of the stairs, looking up at me. He later told me, "You appeared to be floating with the biggest smile on your face, and you looked like you were ten feet tall and that all was well in your world!" (He got it half-right: I'm five-foot; he's six-three.)

After talking with my Laser buddies, I got my "ratchet" and went outside to my boat and "played" with my new toy. Sure enough, it worked like a charm and right then I imagined I could feel that my fingernails had grown back and my hands felt great already!

As I was out there working on my boat, Jim, the gentleman at the bottom of the stairs, came out to talk to me. We had a nice conversation and he left to take his new 16-foot Hobie Cat catamaran home.

I had some friends over that evening and told them that I had met this nice man named Jim. After a short hesitation, I added that I just knew I would hear from him. They asked, "Did you give him your telephone number?" I told them, "No, I didn't, but I know he's going to call."

Well, it just so happened that Jim had gone back and told the owner of the marina that I had given him my telephone number, but he had lost it. After getting the third degree, he gave it to Jim. (It turned out the whole Hobie Cat fleet "clucked" over us and watched our romance blossom until we got married a year later.)

Sure enough, he called and asked me on a date to the Hobie Cat races up in the mountains at the 10,000-foot high Dillon Reservoir. I was delighted to hear from him and accepted the invitation gleefully. When making preliminary plans, what to bring and what to wear, he cautioned me that the water would be cold and the winds brisk and cool. When I asked him if I should bring my wet suit, or at least my wet-pants, he was surprised and asked if I was a scuba-diver. I sure was! The funny part was that we had the same teacher in 1965 at the same diving school and took lessons at the same time, just different classes!

As it turned out, we needed wet-pants. As we raced, we did very well for a change, which Jim said was quite unusual for him since he was still getting used to the boat. We were out in front, going by the grandstand, when a gust of wind coming over the mountain hit the top of our mast and buried one pontoon in the water, making us come to a sudden stop with the bow of that pontoon going into the water and the stern rising up in the air. I was at the jib (the little sail in the front of the boat) and was gently sliding into the water, thinking, "Oh, my, we are having a submarine capsize." I want you to know I had read my Laser sailing book cover-to-cover, had read about the submarine capsize, and knew what was happening to us at that moment.

The winds were still blowing hard in my direction. When Jim, who was holding on and standing on the lower pontoon, kept calling my name, I could hear him but he could not hear me calling back to him because the strong wind was carrying my voice away.

When he could not see or hear me, he was starting to worry that he had lost me and was getting ready to dive to look for me. I realized that he could not see or hear me, so I swam close behind him until he could finally hear me. All he said was, "How in the world did you get behind me?"

Kind of cocky, I told him, "I swam."

He was very glad to see me. Dillon Reservoir is deep and cold. Diving in that environment would not have been fun and most likely not successful!

He pulled me up to stand in front of him on the pontoon in order to add to his weight to break the suction of the big sail lying on the water. Even with my additional hundred pounds, it was still not enough to break the suction and right the boat.

The command boat had to come to lift the top of the mast and break it loose to get it done. Once up, we took off like a shot! That big Hobie sail was fully battened (meaning it was made stiff with individual "battens" throughout the sail) and instantaneously ready to catch the wind full-force as soon as the boat was righted.

Jim had instructed me to be careful when the catamaran came back up, and for me to have my arm over my head so the hull would not hit It. I was to let it push me under then come up immediately to grab the trampoline and get on.

Good instructions! The maneuver went as slick as could be and I got on the trampoline. We proceeded to finish with a great flourish, going by the grandstand and through the finish line to hit the beach. Everyone in the grandstand had witnessed our spectacular submarine capsize and one of our friends came wading out to welcome us with a drink in each hand.

We received a big round of applause. Our first date ended with a big Hobie Cat Race party. What fun! Jim decided I was such a good sport, being dumped into that cold water and coming back up with a big smile on my face, that I was a "keeper." From that day on, we loved being with each other and have been "glued" together ever since.

Jim was a captain in the Navy Reserves at that time. With his Navy experiences, he has, to this day, great respect for the water and the sea. Safety first at all times.

After we got married, I crewed on the Hobie Cat all the time and my beloved Laser sat in the garage. I decided to sell the boat to someone who would appreciate and use it. The marina where I had bought it had a bulletin board and I posted my ad, "Laser for sale! Dearly loved for one season! I married a Hobie Cat!" I sold it to a fellow sailor and was given visiting rights.

Once, we had an unexpected adventure on one of our cruises because of my Laser. When the cruise ship docked at the port of Montevideo, Uruguay, Jim had previously made arrangements to engage a private tour guide and car for the day, and they were waiting for us when we went ashore.

Our guide turned out to be a delightful young lady from a well-to-do family, who showed us Montevideo and the surrounding areas. We had great rapport with her and the driver, so Jim invited them in the afternoon for our customary "German kaffee und kuchen" (coffee and cake), and they took us to a nice café and introduced us to some local pastries. One of them was a milk pudding pie that we loved. She later e-mailed us the recipe and we tried it and loved it.

But our highlight of that day was when she discovered the little gold sailboat pendant I wore. She asked me if I sailed and what I sailed and was enthralled, squealing when I replied, "A Laser!"

She had competed in the Olympics in a Laser and had earned the silver medal for her country. We were beside ourselves when we got to talking about sailboats! We all had such a wonderful day. The cruise line paid the bill on our behalf and the cost was just added to our overall bill at the end of the cruise. The nice part of our arrangement with the guide was that no money was exchanged at the end of the day and it felt like having visited a good friend.

CHAPTER 28:

*Our "Family Honeymoon" Cruising
to South America and Back*

I was married on June 24, 1977, to the love of my life, James Riford Johnston, who was a Captain in the Navy Reserve at the time. Instead of receiving traditional wedding gifts, we made the decision to raise funds for a hydraulic lift-chair to be installed at the Englewood High School in Englewood, Colorado. For additional needed funds, Jim also got several service clubs involved, who were happy to help pay for the hydraulic lift. It was a great help with our students and made things easier for the teachers. Our handicapped program founded by Mary Carpenter and me is being used by the Red Cross as an example all through the United States.

Jim and I started our life together in an unusual way by going on a fourteen-day honeymoon cruise and taking thirteen people from our wedding party along. I made the suggestion to invite my mother- and father-in-law, my youngest daughter, Jacqueline (my older daughter, Eileen, did not want to come since she was expecting her first child), both of Jim's daughters, Beth and Jill, and son, Will, and cousins Mike, Jolene, and Johnny for companionship along on the cruise.

I felt that since wedding guests flew in to Denver from all over the country, it would be a pity for the newlyweds to leave after the ceremony and not spend more time with them. Eight of us left from Denver to Fort Lauderdale, meeting five more on board the MS Sun Viking.

Denver, CO. June 24, 1977. Part of our wedding party before the next day cruise.

We had a wonderful time. On the way, we got Will and his cousin Mike qualified for an open-water scuba-dive in Saint Thomas, Virgin Islands. At our suggestion, both boys had taken scuba-diving classes at home before going on the cruise. It took hours for them to get qualified; we thought the instructors were going to keep them under water for the rest of their lives. They really got a workout, but seemed to enjoy it.

Because we had so many people with us, and most with different last names, it was a challenge for the maitre d' to seat everyone in the dining room. Jim talked to him, explaining the situation of our wedding party and pointing out that no passenger would want to sit at the table with other people's children. The problem was solved when the cruise line graciously agreed to open an extra dining room for us.

The crew of the S.S. Sun Viking took extra care of our "Honeymoon Group." A dining room steward, who was just going to rest and not work on that particular cruise, offered his services when he heard about our honeymoon cruise wedding party. Another young man, who also had planned not to be working on that trip, volunteered to be our busboy. We received fantastic attention and had a wonderful honeymoon. We never regretted taking all of those people along.

My daughter Jacqueline, Jim's daughters Beth and Jill and a cousin, Jolene were at one table for their meals. Jim's son Will and two of Will's cousins Mike and Johnny shared another table. Their dinner choices were terribly monotonous- lobster one night and prime rib the next. Jim and I sat with his parents, Billie and Bim and an older couple that I knew who thought it would be fun to join us.

Jim held muster every morning and every evening to make sure everyone was there and to talk about the days activities. One of the kids favorite activity was watching the sharks eat the left over food and scraps that were dumped every night.

As it turned out, that was the best decision we could have made because not quite two years later, my father-in-law passed away. We still remember how much fun my in-laws had on that cruise, their first one ever! They may have had more fun than we did. The in-laws enjoyed having the opportunity to have their grandchildren around them for two weeks in a relaxed, carefree environment.

The Yamaha motorcycle that Jim and I toured the Colorado Rocky Mountains on

Jim was raised in Michigan a state surrounded by the Great Lakes and filled with smaller lakes. I was raised in Berlin and enjoyed activities around the lakes and rivers there. He was a lifeguard at Camp Dearborn, a large recreation area named after his hometown, Dearborn, MI. He shoveled coal on the Great Lakes Steamships during a summer. I spent years as a Red Cross Water Safety and Handicapped Instructor teaching swimming in Colorado. Jim and I got together in Colorado because of our interest in sailing. We raced catamarans and took a two-week honeymoon cruise with parts of our families. We lived two years aboard a forty-six-foot ketch sailing out of Fort Lauderdale, FL. Presently we live on Whidbey Island about half way between Seattle WA and Victoria, British Columbia in the Puget Sound. Water has been an important part of both of our lives..

CHAPTER 29:

Moved to Fort Lauderdale, Florida to Become a
"Live-Aboard" Couple on our Yacht, "Hingeweht"

In 1978, a year after Jim and I got married, accumulating unpleasant problems emerged caused by Jim's former spouse, affecting his visitation rights and his relationship with his children in general. At that time, because of unresolved problems, Jim left his position as president of the College for Financial Planning, which he had founded under great personal sacrifices in 1965.

As the president of the College for Financial Planning and the first director of the IAFP International Association of Financial Planners) and the ICFP (Institute of Certified Financial Planners)he was one of the founders of a new profession-Professional Financial Planning. The IAFP and the ICFP joined together to form the FPA (financial Planning Association). Eventually the college was sold to Phoenix University. The CFP (Certified Financial Planning) designation which he established is now known worldwide.

Also, the new commanding officer of Jim's Naval Reserve Intelligence unit deliberately overlooked him for a position that he was highly qualified for. The admiral assuming his new position as senior officer brought his own "boys" in along with him, creating difficult situations for those already in the unit.

Jim's professional and personal life was filled with unpleasantness, which, of course, spilled over on to me, too, clouding our relationship and happiness. On top of all that, my former husband (we had been divorced for three years) decided to become friends with Jim's former wife to see how he could help stir up ugly things.

All of this prompted us to rethink our plans for the future. We decided to move and sell our pleasant little home with the wonderful western view of the Colorado Rocky Mountains. We divided our possessions among our combined six children and prepared for a new life. Our shared love of the water and our mutual dream to one day live on a sailboat was the motivating factor for our change. We decided this was a good time to make our dream come true.

Jim and I aboard one of the many cruise ships we enjoyed over the years

We contacted yacht brokers and looked over many brochures of various sailboats offered for sale in the South Florida and Southern

California areas. We had fun narrowing down the offered selections, features, and details of the many advertised sailboats and what our new "home" should have.

Our extreme difference in height made it necessary to look for a boat that accommodated both our needs. We had to "try on" boats as well as cars to see if they would fit both of us.

Jim and I would look over the various brochures at night in bed. He told me that I kept coming back to a Cal 2-46, a roomy forty-six-foot ketch with lots of extra details offered at a price we could easily afford. I remember saying, "Jim, I think this is our boat."

After completing all the necessary chores in Denver, we packed up what we felt was needed to live on a boat and flew to Fort Lauderdale, Florida, to look over our selection.

My first visit to the boat was terribly disappointing. Its condition cried-out for tender, loving care. It was raining hard when we met the broker at the place where the boat was docked—and rain shows how water-tight a boat really is. Because it had been sitting in the rain and damp climate, we found leaks around all the windows in the main salon and generally around all of the openings. The leaks had caused mildew and created a terribly musty smell. What a mess. However, the engine was an 85 hp Perkins diesel, which, surprisingly, was in good shape and had been well maintained.

We arrived at a mutually satisfactory price with the seller, a doctor from St. Louis. After the vessel was assayed we were told that it was sound but needed two new fuel tanks, which the seller was obliged to pay for, as well as some cosmetic work. We took the boat into a boatyard up the New River in Ft. Lauderdale, where the necessary repairs and replacements were made to our satisfaction. Not knowing the boat's response to certain maneuvers, our first docking in a crowded environment at the boatyard was an interesting challenge.

We took the opportunity to add needed electronics and other improvements, as well as installing air conditioning and a heat pump, which gave us comfort. The water supply for the boat was carried in a stainless steel tank, and the Hingeweht's fuel tanks gave her the capacity to go on engine power for a thousand miles, if needed.

The Cal 2-46 was a center-cockpit vessel. We were pleased to find that the floor plan was configured to accommodate a large, stand-up engine room, which was unusual on sailboats. It housed a freestanding engine, automatic pilot, an easily reached sea cock to control the bilge water, a large workbench accommodating various tools, and the necessary banks of batteries. Maintaining the engine was a pleasure compared to having to open the floorboards in the cabin, which was common on most sailboats.

We had an experienced man named Davy Jones manage the up-keep of the engine and take care of other mechanical needs. The light and airy engine room had its own hatch and ladder, which could be used for ventilation and light as well as an entrance or exit. The door to and from the engine room led into a walk-through passageway with the salon forward on one end and the aft cabin where the master bed-room was located on the other end.

The passageway had its own portholes providing light. It housed a five-foot-long and three-foot-deep freezer unit and offered additional counter space and cabinets.

The main salon forward included our galley (kitchen), dining room (a table with cushioned benches that could be transformed into a dou-ble bed, when needed), and lockers for food, etc.; forward of the salon was a V-berth cabin.

The master suite was large with a full bed (Jim and I learned to sleep "spooned" and turned in unison when necessary) and a long set-tee, which converted easily to a single bed by lifting the back rest. The suite had four portholes, a hatch, and its own head, which we con-verted to a push button flushing system. I just refused to depend on a "pump" for that necessity. We did leave the forward second head with the original pump system in case of electricity failure.

Hanging locker space was not too plentiful but we managed. There was room for all we needed, including Jim's dress uniforms and my evening dresses. We had our television set securely fastened, facing the settee and our bed, and enjoyed watching it in comfort.

The salon, with its many large windows, was a bright and a pleasant place to be. The galley area was compact and equipped to be usable while sailing in a "heeled" (leaning) position. The stove was gimbaled, meaning it stayed horizontal no matter what position the boat was in. The cooking pots could be fastened to the burners to avoid any sliding in rough seas. The cook, at a time of need, could strap him/herself to the different counter areas while preparing meals.

The navigation system was also designed to be used in any weather. Forward of it, and by stepping down into a little entry area, was the second head and shower, and led to the second cabin forward with its V-shaped double bed, a hanging locker, and a hatch.

The interior was all teak. The cabin sole was covered by a removable red carpet, continuing our red, white, and blue color scheme. It gave us a cozy, home-like feeling.

Traditionally, sailors believe it is bad luck to change the name of a ship when a new owner takes over, but that didn't bother us. Before we moved to Ft. Lauderdale, we were talking over dinner about a name for her (all ships seem to be a "she"). Jim wanted a German name and gave me some English words to translate into German. He wanted words that had something to do with the wind or the water. I came up with a word that means "blown there by the wind." Jim asked me to spell it and when I did ("hingeweht"), he said, "That's it! See, it has your name in it!" ("Inge"). The Hingeweht was registered with the U.S. Coast Guard in case we wanted to do some serious international sailing, which would assure us their help and protection if needed.

The Hingeweht was a safe, reliable, full-keel sailing vessel. At times when I was at the helm, with Jim setting the sails just right to catch a good, maximum wind and my steering her to find the best course available right then, I could bring her to sail at a speed of nine knots. Her speed capability was listed at eight knots. What fun! Jim and I are still a good team to this day; we are still "catching the best winds."

True racing sailors would disdainfully call the Hingeweht a motorsailor. But for us, she was home sweet home. Jim was always responsible for the sails and I was at the helm. The two of us could handle her well even in and through Hurricane David in 1980.

The CAL 2-46 was an ideal live-aboard boat. It was comfortable for Jim at six-three and me at five feet. We moved on board and I cleaned and scrubbed everything, and painted the inside of all the lockers. Some were so deep that I had to climb into them. Jim would look for me and call my name, and my response was to stick my hand straight up out of the locker until he found me.

The boat had been outfitted with quality red, white, and blue accessories inside and out. Included were dishes, flatware, placemats, linens, and blankets. Being a naturalized citizen and proudly calling myself a "fierce" American, I still favor and use these colors as often as possible to proclaim my patriotism.

The Hingeweht's safety features were outstanding. We had a portable life boat and canister to store it in, life buoys, life rings, a flare gun, and a radio detection device we could use for others to locate us in emergencies. We carried spare parts for the engine and other equipment and had a spare rudder and helm for emergency steering.

The connections for all of the hoses that discharged water through the hull were changed from simple metal clamps to serious through-hull connections with handles like regular water faucets, if we needed to shut them off.

I was obsessed with installing sea cocks! Imagine sailing along in rough weather and one of the light aluminum clamps breaks or comes loose! The emergency procedure then is to look for and find the right-size teak cone, which was on board and available in different sizes. While the ocean water is gushing in, you are to hammer the teak cone into the hole, which, if done correctly, stops the water from coming in—in effect, stopping the ocean from devouring your boat and you along with it! I certainly could not imagine such a feat and did not want to ever be in a position to find out if that theory worked.

We had plenty of life preservers on board and two special horse-shoe- shaped ones with the name "Hingeweht" on them, fastened on the aft railing. We added a heavy duty, eight-person Avon life raft contained in a capsule on the aft deck. When kicked overboard in an emergency, the capsule would open automatically, providing a life raft with a full canopy and a zipper to provide complete shelter against sun, salt water spray, and inclement weather. Its equipment included survival gear, powerful emergency lights, mirrors, salt water distiller, food, and a built-in beacon for search and rescue to locate the drifting life boat.

As a retired Navy captain, having spent many years at sea, Jim has due respect for Mother Nature and the powers of the mighty oceans of the world. He did not take any unnecessary chances or put others into questionable situations. No one says lightly, "I trust him with my life"—well, I trusted Jim with my life and so did many guests who were with us as our guests during our two-year adventure.

We lived on board just as we would have done had we been living in a house. Certainly we had all the comforts of home. We were prepared for any situation we might have had to face, just as we would have been living on land. In one picture, you can see us getting off our boat; I am wearing a long evening gown and Jim is wearing a white tux on our way to the Navy League's Valentine party.

Jim and I leaving "home" for a Navy League's Valentine's Day Dance Party

When in port, we had guests for dinner or would take them out for lunches, docking right at the restaurant along the Intercoastal Waterway in Fort Lauderdale. We had some funny adventures doing that. Jim always tried to have our "land lubber" guests actively involved in some of the necessary docking activities, if possible. They were usually thrilled to be able to enjoy and participate in all the facets of being on a sailboat.

One of our memorable docking moments included taking two couples to our favorite restaurant, located on the Intercoastal Waterway. There was a certain procedure necessary to dock our boat and we had practiced it all the time. Jim would bring the boat close to the dock so that I could jump down and be ready to receive the line thrown to me from the bow to fasten to a cleat on the dock. Then I would go quickly down the dock and catch the aft line to fasten it to another cleat.

Picture this: It's a great, sunny day, and we approach our landing site in front of a beautiful restaurant on the canal in Ft. Lauderdale. There is a large deck adjoining the open walls of the dining room. People are sitting there, enjoying lunch and watching boats go by—or, like us, watching you dock for lunch.

Captain Jim had assigned the bow line to a friend, who happened to be a retired colonel in the army. He had no nautical knowledge or experience at all, but was instructed what to do. He was shown the line to be tossed, where to stand, and to be ready when the time came to throw the line to me. When his big moment came, he grabbed all of the coiled line without hesitation and threw it to me. Good job!

Except he had forgotten two important details: one, to fasten the end of the line to the cleat on the boat, and, two, to put the line under the safety line to the outside of the boat and then throw it to me. I stood there surprised and somewhat embarrassed in front of the restaurant audience. I watched the Hingeweht maneuver in the swift current, get free, go out again, and turn around for another attempt to dock while I stood there waiting. Well, what can you expect from the army, right? The second attempt to dock proceeded flawlessly. Yeah, Army!

The guests of the restaurant who had been watching gave us a cheer when we finally docked. By the time we all sat down for lunch, we were hungry and had certainly earned our meal. I bet our audience thought we were bloody beginners! I am glad to report that our guests were oblivious to the spectacle we made while docking. Those things happen to the best of sailors.

When we met other boaters, we always exchanged stories and pointers on where to go, where to anchor, and that sort of thing. I was told many times during these conversations that some of them had bought a lot of real estate in certain places. I thought that was nice and was happy for them until Jim took me aside and said, "'Buying real estate' means running aground."

I know how that felt because a few times when we ran aground we just had to sit there until the tide came back in to "free" us. Once, Jim's youngest son, Will, and his friend Steve came to visit. True to his philosophy, Jim made them feel welcome and let Steve take the helm while we were heading down toward Miami on the Intercostal Waterway. The channels are fairly narrow all through Florida's waterways and anyone at the helm has to constantly watch the depth meter.

Jim got distracted and just missed a moment watching Steve at the helm. Steve drifted out of the channel and ran aground. He offered to jump into the water to see what we were hung up on. As he jumped in, we were laughing when he came up, standing on a rock. The Hingeweht needed five feet to float and there we were, bouncing up and down on solid coral rock. Motorboats came by looking and wondering what we were doing in that unlikely spot. Finally, a big Hatteras motorboat came by and was powerful enough to pull us free.

Every time we had guests on board, Jim performed a "man overboard drill" as soon as we got into the Gulf Stream outside of Port Everglades. He would throw a life preserver overboard. One of his objectives was to teach everyone to be a lookout and keep their eyes on the object in the water. The helmsman always checked the compass reading so we could return on an exact reference of 180 degrees from the original heading where the "man overboard" accident occurred. He always stressed that everyone on board is a lookout when there is a "man overboard."

Many times, before we could even begin our recovery maneuver, a motor boat with individuals aboard who wanted to be helpful would pick up the life preserver and race after us waving wildly to bring it back to us. Jim would tell everyone not to mention to our "good Samaritans" that we threw it overboard on purpose, in order to not make them feel bad.

We loved our boat and I cried when we sold her. She was in perfect condition and when she was assayed for the sale, no recommendations or requests were made to change, repair, or replace anything. That fact was most unusual in the boat-selling business.

Our cherished memories of having lived for two wonderful years on our boat are up near the top of my "unbelievable adventures.' It was the fulfillment of a wonderful lifelong dream that we both had long before we met!

CHAPTER 30:

Aboard the Hingeweht, during Hurricane David, in the "Eye" and All

When one reads in the newspapers, sees on television, or hears on the radio about Hurricane David or Sophia or whatever its name is threatening the South Florida coast and that alerts have been posted to take precautions, most people don't pay attention.

I assure you, however, that those near the hurricane location or in its potential path, whether they are on dry land or at sea, pay great attention to hurricanes. The imminent danger must be dealt with. One particular adventure involves our intimidating encounter with such a hurricane force.

Jim and I survived Hurricane David in 1980 on our Cal 2-46 ketch, Hingeweht, in South Florida waters, though it began in Fort Lauderdale. When the hurricane warning was broadcast, we were fortunate enough to be able to immediately leave our dock on the Isle of Venice and head to a Hurricane Hole for safety. Hurricane holes are usually inland from the ocean and provide shelter of some sort from the winds and wild waves; they also have solid holding bottoms for anchors. Our choices were to sail either south and find a spot in the Florida Keys, or north and seek a hideaway in one of the inland bays. We chose a hurricane hole in San Piper Bay, north of Palm Beach, up a good-size river, because it had an eight-foot depth, not much of a tide, and the bottom was laced with mango roots that made anchoring safe.

The canals around Fort Lauderdale were popular and in great demand for dock rentals because they are deep enough to accommodate sailboats with five- to six-foot drafts. They also had easy access to the Inter Coastal Waterway a north-south waterway from South Florida all the way up the East Coast to New York.

We had leased dock space on the Isle-of-Venice, which was a beautiful place to call home for the Hingeweht, even if "home" was only a space by the dock. There are handsomely landscaped homes along the canals that were a pleasure to look at. We were proud to be a part of that neighborhood with our beautiful yacht.

We had been keeping track of Hurricane David and when we heard the actual alert, we knew it was time to leave. One does not want to be in a canal or moored to a dock during a hurricane. The pilings separating the boats become instant hazards; following a hurricane, the feared water surges, five to ten feet high, can lift boats out of the water, impale them on pilings, or smash them on the dock or into another boat.

It's usually a requirement in these areas to evacuate people and boats, creating big traffic jams, partly because the many drawbridges on the Inter Coastal Waterway have to be opened for sailboats and large motorboats to get through, which stops all car traffic across them and makes evacuations doubly difficult. On the same note, boats of all kinds are in the canals, trying to move away from the hurricane's path.

I had cleaned up the yacht, vacuumed, and dusted before we left the dock while Hurricane David was still at sea but approaching South Florida. Not knowing what to expect, I did not want to have to worry about a dirty boat. Jim thought that was very funny.

We beat the biggest onslaught of boats going north on the Inter-Coastal, though it was terribly crowded and slow-moving. It was so slow that we decided to sail "outside" in the ocean, hoping to move north faster, especially with the Gulf Stream helping us. It was gutsy of us because of the increasing strength of the wind, which helped increase the size of the waves as well. But as it turned out, we were able to move along faster.

We sailed in the ocean all by ourselves. There wasn't another boat in sight. The ocean was eerie and we had never before seen so many different and unexplainable water textures and movements around us. Our Perkins diesel engine steadily pushed us north through the Gulf Stream against the ever-increasing winds; the clouds looked like the bottom of big copper kettle drums.

I was at the helm. Jim was busy securing all sails and booms, and moving everything else he could below deck. The less wind resistance, the safer the boat in a hurricane; the only wind resistance left was the boat's hull, deck house, and two bare masts.

As we reached the Palm Beach inlet, the winds were declared "hurricane strength," which was in the 75 mph range. It prompted us to immediately seek shelter, which meant going inland. The Palm Beach inlet was not one of our favorites for going inland because of its difficult configuration, poor markings, and narrowness, but nevertheless it was a welcome sight. I was still at the helm with Jim continuing to strip the deck of anything moveable.

I remember my feelings of dread while holding tightly on to the helm when we decided to go into the Palm Beach inlet and away from the angry ocean. I still recall barely being able to see the narrow, winding inlet, having to contend with the increasing winds, and having to overcome the extremely poor visibility, making it difficult to find the markers to be able to go into that inlet "on range."

"On range" navigation is an interesting concept. Since I could not see a marked channel to follow, I had to motor slowly until I found and could line up two range markers. I kept slowly motoring along until I had one marker lined up in front of the other, so that the first one covered the second until it appeared to be only one range marker. That assured me that I was steering in the right direction and that I was in the deep traffic channel.

While I was concentrating on avoiding running aground in a narrow channel, I still had to contend with the hurricane strength winds buffeting our boat and the poor visibility to make the situation even more difficult. I did get it done and the waterway opened to a wider, marked channel! Captain Jim exclaimed, "Well done" and that I could keep my job as "First Mate." It felt good to be able to relax my hold on the helm.

We motored up the St. Lucie River and found a spot in Sand Piper Bay, isolating us as much as possible from other boats. There were eight to ten boats there when we entered the bay. The next morning, when we awoke, we found at least twice that many, most of which were not manned. Many people anchored their boat in what they considered a safe hurricane hole, but did not want to stay on board during the hurricane. The Hingeweht was our home, however, so leaving it during a hurricane was out of the question. A heavy, forty-foot fishing boat had been anchored near us overnight. We had to keep an eye on its swinging back and forth during the hurricane.

We put out two anchors at the bow in a "V" formation; each anchor was marked with one of our buoys so we could constantly check their holding properly. The Hingeweht was a good, sturdy, reliable boat and we felt safe. With the morning came the increase in winds with gusts up to 100 mph. When the wind gusts hit the boat, she would heel over (lean) and then right herself and turn her bow back into the wind. She was doing the heeling and righting herself for hours. That rhythm was comforting and made us feel secure.

Below deck, we had secured all of our important papers with radio beepers in watertight pouches encased with life preservers to make them float, if necessary. We were also wearing life preservers at all times.

Everything inside the cabins was tightly fastened down. It was cozy in our salon and we had nothing more to do, having done all that was necessary under these circumstances, so we played cards. We constantly listened to the marine weather reports, which seemed to indicate that the hurricane was moving to the north, well clear of Florida's eastern coast.

Then, suddenly, we realized that it was totally still—no wind or even a sound! We were in the eye of the hurricane. The Miami maritime weather report told us that the hurricane was well out to sea, traveling in a northerly direction, but they were absolutely wrong. What a sensation! Talk about an eerie feeling! You have to experience it to believe it. Everything seemed gray and black, and the air felt heavy. According to what the constantly monitored weather forecasts were telling us, we were not supposed to be in the hurricane's eye. But, there we were, sitting in it! The realization changed the situation and demanded new strategies from us.

We went on deck and Jim reversed (switched) the anchor lines. He knew that after the eye of a hurricane passed, the winds came from the opposite direction. If the anchor lines were not switched, what had held them tight against the previous winds would not do so with the winds coming the opposite way. Jim's experience with two previous hurricanes on Navy ships had taught him what to expect.

During the lull, while we were in the eye of the hurricane, we were on deck, checking and inspecting things. Jim noticed a sailboat anchored about 100 yards to the south with two young children aboard. We were surprised that parents would expose their children, especially that young, to the danger of being on a sailboat, even anchored, in a hurricane. In addition, we noticed that neither the children nor the parents wore life preservers. Jim said that the captain on that boat was either very dumb or very smart to not allow those on board to wear life preservers during a hurricane. As it turned out, he was dumb!

Their boat had two cabins—one aft for the adults (newlyweds, we found out later), which was where all four people were staying. The other cabin was forward but could be reached only by passing through the center cockpit. All of the radios were in the forward cabin. We understood that a boat anchored behind them was trying to radio them that their anchor was slipping and their boat drifting. But *they* were in the aft cabin with their children and out of radio contact. Most likely, they had not even monitored the weather reports.

When the wind came up again, we could not believe our eyes. That sailboat had started up and was heading out of the bay. Dumb!

The man at the helm looked dazed and appeared to be in shock. He was hunched forward, with hands locked tightly on the helm, and was neither looking left nor right. Jim hollered out to him, "Hey, watch what you're doing! You're running over our anchor lines!" But there was no response. We stood helplessly by, watching a disaster in progress! He stayed on that course and ran over both of our anchor lines, which slowed him down. Jim started the engines on the Hingeweht and backed down, trying to avoid the inevitable.

His boat worked its way up our anchor lines until both boats smacked together. We were hopelessly entangled. The rest was a blur until we were beached, heeled over on our port (left) side in about three feet of water. Because of the tangled situation, his boat was against ours, pointed in the same direction and also heeled over.

We had a five-foot draft on our boat. Jim checked to see if we were okay then jumped overboard and tied the Hingeweht's main mast to a big palm tree high up on the beach. That was in case of a water surge, which could lift the water level up ten extra feet.

Jim hollered at the other boat's captain, "You better get your kids off your boat in case of a surge." He didn't know what "surge" meant, though he did as Jim suggested.

Jim also insisted that they wear life preservers. He told the older girl (probably about eight) to talk to her younger brother, who had some physical handicaps. Jim tied them to a tree, giving them room to wander a bit but not too far, and explained to them that he did that to keep them safe and that they should stay there until their folks came to pick them up.

Their mother was a sight. She wore just panties and a t-shirt. She looked like she was in a wet t-shirt contest!

We exchanged information, which Jim did a lot more peacefully than I would have! Then we decided to stay and sleep that first night on our boat just for safekeeping. However, trying to sleep on a boat with a forty-degree heel was impossible so, after the first night, we took lodging in the nearby Sandpiper Bay Hotel.

The next morning, we discovered that our rubber life raft had been stolen but that one of our anchors was still on a taught line aft of our boat and its dragging effect probably kept us from being beached much further up the beach, creating a lot of damage. We did lose the other anchor, however, so we radioed the Coast Guard for help, but they said they could not help unless there was a danger of life or limb.

The presumed owner of the other boat made arrangements to have his boat pulled off. He continued to display an overwhelming ignorance of the usual procedure when pulling off a sailboat from shore into deeper water. The company hired to do the salvage job suggested that they just flip his boat onto the other side, which would put his keel toward the beach. By tying a strong rope to the top of the mast then pulling the rope away from the beached boat, it could gently pull her out, thus avoiding any further damage.

"Oh, no!" he said. "This is a brand-new boat and no one is going to do that to it."

Little did this inexperienced sailor know that the procedure has been used for hundreds of years. So the rescue company did the only other choice: They blasted a channel through the coral wide enough to pull the sailboat out without flipping it over.

It took the salvage company three days and when they did get it pulled off, the stern came free first and swung around to hit the Hingeweht on its starboard (right) side, putting a hole in the hull. Luckily for us it was above the waterline. Now we had no engine power because the prop was torn off, we had lost one anchor, a dingy was stolen, and we had sustained a big hole in the hull.

I always say there is something good to something bad. Not having to worry about getting water in the boat, we flipped it over from the right side to the left, so the keel could be dragged rather than pushed, and hauled her off in less than an hour. No big deal. The other boat should have been flipped that way also. It would have been a lot less hassle and expense.

We did manage to locate a good boatyard close to Sand Piper Bay. We were the first casualties contacting them so we were towed to their yard immediately. The Hingeweht was there in dry dock for three months. We paid $25,000 in cash (1980 currency) up front for repairs. Neither insurance company had given us any help.

We also paid three months for dock space in Fort Lauderdale so we would not lose it and we rented a condominium in Fort Pierce for the time it took to get our baby shipshape. As the saying in the boating business goes, "No cash, no splash!" Our payouts seemed to be a never-ending process. It wasn't supposed to be that way, however, since both boats were insured.

Every time we visited the Hingeweht in dry dock to check on the progress, I cried. The workmen kept assuring me that they would make her like new again. Eventually they did, but not without more trials and tribulations.

The boat had to be repainted three times. The first coat was fine but after the second coat it rained before the paint dried. To avoid further rain damage, they put the Hingeweht into a large covered shed and painted her again. This time the driving rain came *sideways* into the open entrance of the shed, hitting the fresh paint. She had to be sanded and painted for the third time, but ended up looking beautiful!

We had the main mast removed and painted during the other repairs. We also had the spar lights replaced and the old radio antenna on top of the mast switched to a flexible one. Taking the opportunity while the Hingeweht was in dry dock, we also had the cooking stove in the galley removed and I took it to a special company for reconditioning.

It was a gimbaled propane stove, meaning its construction enabled it to stay vertical no matter how much the boat heeled one way or the other. It also had stainless steel rails to secure cooking pots in the vertical, so that cooking could continue regardless of what the boat was doing. With that convenience, good meals were always available.

When the Hingeweht was finally launched, it was in perfect condition. The workers and craftsmen had kept their word.

We happily boarded the Hingeweht to take her back home to Fort Lauderdale. It had been three months since the hurricane and we were anxious to get our lives back to normal. The weather had been unstable after the hurricane and the tides were abnormally high and low. There was one fixed bridge over the St. Lucie River that we had to go under. We knew it would be a close fit with our mast sixty-three feet above the waterline, so we waited for dead low tide before proceeding under the bridge. Still, we knew it would be tight.

Just before going under the bridge, Jim had the engine in slow reverse (while I was praying) so we could back down quickly in case of a mishap. Holding our breath, we proceeded. Looking up, we saw our flexible antenna bend way back and we heard "click, click, click" as it ran along the steel girders supporting the bridge. We heard the clicking all the way through.

We breathed deeply for the first time after we reached the other side of the bridge and saw the sky again.

Replacing the old, straight antenna with a new, flexible one had been a good move. There were two or three more bridges we needed to go under on a higher tide than normal, but they all opened for us when we blew our horn. Bless the bridge masters and the bridges they control!

When we had exchanged insurance information with the inexperienced boat owner, little did we know what we were in for. All the information he gave us was incorrect except for his name and the fact that the boat was insured by Lloyd's of London.

He did not own the boat. One corporation, owned by another corporation, owned by yet another corporation, was the apparent owner.

It was totally confusing and probably deliberately so. The boat captain told us he was a retired lawyer and CIA agent.

All through the repair period, we did not hear from Lloyd's of London. Jim called, asking for the president. Whoever responded checked their files and, yes, the boat was insured by them, but they were surprised to hear from us because no report had been filed about the accident. So they sent an agent to see our boat and we were concerned because his evaluation would be made after it had undergone some repairs.

Our challenge? The offending boat, with its four-person crew, had left the country and no one knew where it went. It became necessary for us to sue for recovery, but how does one serve papers to a boat owner when he and his boat are in international waters and you cannot find them?

It's funny how various life experiences serve you well when you least expect it. Jim's last command in the Navy was as commanding officer of a Navy Intelligence unit. He used his experience in intelligence work to track the boat around various ports in the international waters of the Caribbean and finally back to Palm Beach, Florida.

He did this by staying in touch with the boatyard where the boat had been purchased. When it needed parts or maintenance, the boatyard would let Jim know the boat's location. It was over two years from the day of the accident that papers could be served and a court date set.

The court appearance was an experience for me. Jim whispered, while we were seated in the courtroom, "Inge, look at all the people here: the Judge, the bailiff, the recorder, a police guard, two lawyers, and the two of us. We are the only ones *not* getting paid." It amazed me. I had never sued someone or was ever in a situation like this before.

As the trial proceeded, I thought it was all done because the judge had just said, "Case dismissed!" and I was ready to leave. Jim told me that just the case brought against *us* had been dismissed. We had been counter-sued for being anchored and in the way of the boat that hit us. I could not believe the stupidity of such a frivolous lawsuit, warranting all the manpower and expense! The saying "live and learn" came to me then.

We spent three more hours sitting in court, listening to unbeliev-ably irrelevant and inconsequential questions like, "Where did you buy the dinghy that was stolen?" and "Which one did you buy first, the dingy or the life raft?" I can't remember all the stupid questions asked, but none had anything to do with having been hit by a boat with an in-competent skipper at the helm who, by the way, did not appear for the court date even though he was forced to write a deposition.

When parts of the deposition were read, the boat owner was asked what action he took while sitting in the eye of the hurricane. He said he didn't know what that meant. A specific question asked of him was, "Did you change your anchor lines?" He answered, "Why?" I thought it was all over and I was leaving. He sure made a fool of himself after proclaiming he was an experienced captain.

We were awarded our full $25,000 but received no interest be-cause the insurance company's lawyer did not file for it. When we were told by our insurance company to go to our lawyer's office to pick up our check, we discovered that it was only half the amount of our claim.

The lawyer claimed that half of the $25,000 was his fee. Jim called the president of the Insurance Company of North America because of my concern about the total unfairness, and got right through to him. The president asked only one question, "Did you sign a separate con-tract with this lawyer?" When we told him no, he said he'd call back. We got his return call within minutes and he advised us to go and get our check in the full amount.

That lawyer must have thought we were easy pickings. I suspect that bright but foolish young man lost his affiliation with INA right then and there. At least, I hope he did.

Jim and I always seem to weather the storms not only of life in general but life at sea and in the courtroom.

CHAPTER 31:

In the Ft. Lauderdale Navy League

When we lived on the yacht, Jim was the secretary of the Ft. Lauderdale Navy League and actively involved in all of their functions, which, of course, also involved me. The mission of Navy League members included greeting the U.S. Navy ships and all foreign Navy ships that made Fort Lauderdale one of their ports-of-call. It was a pleasure to meet and welcome the officers and crews of many nationalities. My being bilingual in English and German came in handy many times.

It was a once-in-a-lifetime experience when Jim (Navy Captain James R. Johnston, former commanding officer of a Navy Intelligence unit at Patrick Air Force Base in Central Florida) received an invitation to dine on board the Royal Navy's airplane carrier, "The Illustrious," which was en route back to England from the Falkland Islands after the British-Argentina conflict in 1982.

Jim was being honored for the help his unit provided to Great Britain during that conflict. It seemed that the Royal Navy had sustained heavy casualties, including the loss of the destroyer Sheffield, because they were not able to successfully defend their ships against the Execet missiles. The information provided by Jim's unit turned the tide in their favor and was not forgotten when the opportunity presented itself to meet U.S. Navy Captain James R. Johnston, who was responsible for having helped them succeed.

Captain J.C.K. Slater made a humorous speech, along with presenting a handmade plaque, which had been carved on board by a sailor who had been involved in the Falkland Island War. He concluded his remarks with the comment, "As a whole, we do not recognize the colonists but, on this occasion, we will make an exception."

Jim, in turn, presented a "You Are Welcome" plaque to the captain on behalf of himself and the members of his unit.

The dinner was great, and Jim and I were treated royally. The special meal made for that occasion was excellent and spiked with famous British specialties like trifle. The tour through the Illustrious was also interesting. This ship was a "ski-jump carrier," so called because the deck where airplanes took off and landed was not flat like those on board U.S. aircraft carriers, but was constructed just like a ski jump in reverse.

At the dinner, we were introduced to their young "ace" pilot and I asked him what his profession was in civilian life. I was taken aback when he replied, "Concert pianist." His response to my surprised expression was a shrug of the shoulder and, "I just love to fly."

That entire occasion was a great adventure for me and I was so proud of Jim, especially after hearing all the once-classified information involved in that war.

Another special, memorable adventure came about when we greeted the officers and crew of U. S. Nuclear Attack Submarine Hammerhead making port in Fort Lauderdale. Once it became known that Jim was a retired Navy captain, he was immediately invited to join the skipper of the submarine on board for dinner. We received a restricted tour of the submarine that included an underway trip at a depth of about 400 feet. What a thrill for me to embark on yet another unbelievable adventure when I was included in the invitation!

As a retired senior officer, Jim was honored by being asked to join the commanding officer on the submarine's bridge while it departed and returned to Port Everglades. We also had an exquisite dinner served in the small officers' mess at 400 feet below sea level, at a table beautifully set with white table linens, napkins, and special china reserved for guests. We were served by professionally trained stewards and Jim asked to meet and personally thank the cook afterwards for preparing such a wonderful meal for us.

As the only female guest, I was treated to taking a look through the telescope. I saw a freighter steaming toward Port Everglades and asked the skipper if that freighter would know we were below looking at him. He replied, "I hope not."

I was also permitted to shoot air charges as though they were torpedoes. What an experience! Each sailor I met everywhere we went on the brief tour was proud to explain to me what his job was on the submarine. I was awed at the efficiency of everything.

When I needed to use the "facility," the captain graciously offered me the head (toilet) in his quarters, which I gladly accepted. When I was trying to flush, I looked around and all I could find were two big wheels, no buttons or pump. Those wheels were huge! I thought I'd better not turn them because I might do something wrong and "sink" the boat. Afterwards, I wondered how one goes about "sinking" a submarine that was already 400 feet down!

To my embarrassment, I had to ask someone to please take care of the flushing for me. I was so intimidated by those wheels that I did not want to be shown how they worked! To my relief, that situation was handled graciously. Yet another unbelievable adventure—and another wonderful experience added to my life story.

To show our appreciation for the extraordinary hospitality, Jim invited the captain and a few of his officers and crew to be our guests on board our fifty-foot yacht, the Hingeweht. If we thought we were excited to be on the Hammerhead, you should have seen these hardened seafarers' excitement coming aboard the Hingeweht!

We picked them up alongside the Hammerhead; it was a trick maneuver getting close to her low, bulging hull, but we managed. It was fun—with a lot of jokes and laughter—as we helped them aboard. They enjoyed the trip and the chance to sail *on top* of the water.

It was a special treat for the submariners to motor along the Inter-Coastal Waterway, which is actually the only way to see the unobstructed views of the fabulous mansions of the rich and famous, as well as the homes of sheiks and other well-to-do people.

They were eager to participate in our request, asking the bridge masters to open the bridges for us by tooting our horn or using a powerful spotlight to shine directly into the bridge tenders' office above the bridge. They did so manually, and it was an interesting, new experience for them.

We became friends with the captain and his lady, and were mutually delighted when we met them again at an Armed Forces Ball at the Air Force Academy in Colorado Springs, Colorado. We learned later that he became the superintendent of the Naval Academy.

CHAPTER 32:

The Kangaroo Lady's
Unbelievable Christmas Adventures

When is a refrigerator an adventure? Only when it involves one of my favorite gratifying experiences!

After we sold the Hingeweht, our beloved floating home for two years, in the early 1980s, Jim and I opened a nutritional counseling practice and health supplement shop called "To Your Good Health," in Pompano Beach, Florida. Our counseling approach involved incorporating nutrition, health, and life enhancement. Our concept was unique and we became well known for our health knowledge.

We also fulfilled our joint desire to make a difference in people's life. We used our lifestyle and knowledge to educate, help, and nurture the many middle-aged people and senior citizens we attracted. We were astounded at how many lonesome and unhappy people lived in South Florida.

Many had given up their homes and moved away from long-time friends and relatives. Their thinking was that they would find a sunny and warm paradise in South Florida and live happily ever after. The reality was that people just like themselves sought the same dream, but were unable to replace their long-time friends and caring relatives. Getting connected was difficult because lonesome and unhappy people do not make good companions, friends, or neighbors.

We met and helped all kinds of people in the work we did. Some of them were well-to-do, some just getting by in life, and some poor. Spending our first Christmas on land after two years "at sea" aboard the Hingeweht, we decided to share our good fortune and make Christmas happier for others.

Our focus was to collect Christmas gifts and distribute them to others. Jim made this known with a few press releases that stirred up interest. When we then made it known that Santa was at work in our shop collecting Christmas gifts, toys, and food, we were overwhelmed by the generosity of our community volunteering to help.

Gifts of teddy bears, dolls, and money were brought in regularly (especially by those who did not have the time to get involved gave us money). People realized that Christmas-giving projects like ours always took financial aid, and they were willing to provide it.

Living in a warm climate, I always wore a cool jumpsuit with a bib pocket on the front of my chest. People would say, "Inge, I do not have time to buy a gift. Please get one for me or use the money wherever you think it is needed."

I would thank them and put the money or check right into my bib pocket. I sometimes felt like a kangaroo with my pocket stuffed so full.

As we kept on receiving monetary gifts, we realized we had enough to further expand our efforts. We broadened our approach, adding food baskets to the children's gifts. Jim approached the manager of the supermarket in our small plaza, who agreed to sell us turkeys at reduced prices. That way they felt they were part of the Christmas-giving spirit. We were excited to be able to include a turkey and all the trimmings in each basket, making life a lot easier and Christmas a lot merrier for a number of families.

The Christmas spirit was catching on and the whole project became such a heart-warming endeavor that it attracted a great many people in and around Pompano Beach. It was creating a ripple effect, which made all those who got involved feel good to be part of such generosity.

This is where the refrigerator comes in. As I mentioned, we had many different people coming to our counseling practice and health food store. We never knew who would be there at any one time. One day, while I was talking to a mother of five children, who had come to ask me for some toys for them, I asked if she was going to have a turkey for Christmas.

"No," she said, "I don't think I can afford one."

I offered to provide her with a Christmas turkey for her family then asked if she had a stove with an oven to roast the turkey.

"Yes," she said, "I do. But I have no refrigerator."

I could not imagine how a family with five children, living in hot Southern Florida, was able to survive without a refrigerator. I asked her how she managed to keep the milk from spoiling. She replied, as a matter of fact, that she bought whatever was needed daily.

Well! I told her I would get her a refrigerator for Christmas! Jim just looked at me and said "How?" I did not know at that moment, but I knew I would.

As it turned out, I got two offers of a refrigerator on the same day! We even had a choice, and selected the one with the self-defrosting feature for her.

One of our customers had overheard me talking to the young mother and came back later to tell me that he was going to surprise his wife with a new refrigerator for Christmas and that I could have the one being replaced for the mother in need.

I knew then that God was helping me help a needy person have a happier Christmas. We made arrangements when and where to pick up the refrigerator, and also when to be at the home of the family receiving it. We even found a truck and two strong men who offered to help with the moving and transportation. It turned out that getting it there was not a problem. It was miraculous how everything fell into place.

The big refrigerator adventure continued. When we got to the home to pick it up, we found a very surprised and befuddled young wife frantically emptying and cleaning out her old refrigerator. We were standing there with a truck and several men, waiting for her to finish so we could take it. There were also two deliverymen standing alongside us, waiting to deliver her new Christmas refrigerator.

Everyone waiting, however, was in good spirits and assured her that she was doing a good job. Her husband enjoyed how the whole project was developing and how dramatic a surprise his Christmas gift for his wife had turned out to be. He never dreamed it would involve all of the volunteers and end up making a family he did not know unexpectedly happy because of the refrigerator that was coming their way.

The rest was easy. The used refrigerator was moved out of the house and onto the truck then proceeded to the neighborhood where our young family lived. Picture this: The truck was first, with its gleaming refrigerator standing proudly in the back for all to see, carefully driving down the street to its destination, followed by a small caravan of volunteers in their cars.

The street where the refrigerator was to be taken was lined on both sides with people waiting to see the new appliance delivered to their neighbor. A parade could not have attracted more people! That lovingly given gift became the big attraction of the neighborhood and ended up receiving the place of honor in its new home. Where? In the living room, the most popular place where all could see and enjoy it.

In addition to the beautiful refrigerator, this young family received a turkey with all the trimmings and wrapped gifts for each of the five children, as well as for Mom and Dad and maybe, if needed, for a grandmother. In addition, our First United Methodist Church gave each family member an outfit of their choice from the church thrift shop.

All together, we filled sixty-five food baskets, including sixty-five turkeys. Each of the sixty-five families also received additional gifts for each family member. Just imagine all of those baskets and extra gifts lined up in a row in the church meeting hall! What an awesome sight! It was an 'unbelievable adventure' for all involved!

I was fortunate that my sister-in-law, Kay, offered to help put it all together. It got so big that we had to take over the church meeting hall. Long tables filled the hall where the sixty-five baskets were being assembled. We marked each one with the family name and the names of each family member. We even made special efforts to put the one special gift that each child had wished for and had written to Santa Clause requesting it in the basket.

Oh! It was a glorious, blessed Christmastime and the spirit of giving spread wider and wider, making small miracles possible.

CHAPTER 33:

More Christmas Adventures

Fully dressed in his traditional red suit, except for wearing red Bermuda shorts in deference to the warm weather in South Florida, Santa Claus was portrayed by one of our faithful Methodist church members. He was devoted to making our Christmas project a huge success when he arrived on the back of a good, reliable truck loaded with beautifully wrapped gifts and a bicycle.

Santa explained to the big-eyed children gathered in a large group why he arrived on a truck and not in his sleigh pulled by reindeer. He told them he did not want to disappoint them by not getting any gifts to them because he could not use his sleigh in Florida; hence, he used this truck.

He further explained, "The reindeer did not want to go where it was hot and there was no snow."

Then he asked if they were happy that he came, even though it was by truck. Noisily, they assured him that he did the right thing and that they were very happy.

It was exciting to see over a hundred smiling children getting gifts directly from Santa. The little boy who had asked Santa for a bicycle (since his had been stolen) was especially happy. He again could deliver his newspapers and not disappoint his customers.

It was a festive occasion and we celebrated with punch and Christmas cookies. We sang Christmas carols and felt happy and blessed to all be there together. We still had more gifts to deliver, and the children understood. After many hugs and kisses, they waved goodbye to us.

It was getting dark and Jim came with our car and offered to help us deliver the rest of the packages. Our car was stuffed full with the many boxes that our friends at the store in our little shopping center had helped us wrap with beautiful Christmas paper.

When we stopped at the first house on Santa's list, the children were waiting, sitting on the steps of their house under a porch light. When our car stopped, they came running. Jim opened the door and the inside car light went on. All we could see were happy, shining faces and we could hear them saying over and over again, "Are these all for us?"

We assured them that, yes, all of the Christmas packages were for them. Then we carried the gifts into the house, making sure that everyone there received a package with their name on it.

Happiness was glowing on their faces and that happiness was reflected doubly in the eyes of the parents and grandparents, who were able to witness and experience it. We talked a bit then said that we needed to be on our way to deliver more packages.

When we finished, we went back to our church, the First United Methodist Church in Pompano Beach. Santa thanked me for helping make his job so easy and I was happy, thinking about how well everything had worked out. I thanked our "Elf Helpers," especially Jim and Santa, for their help and support on this Christmas project.

I was surprised then, when Jim handed me a big box, saying, "It seems Santa forgot to deliver this one."

When I opened it, I found a beautiful, three-foot cloth doll smiling at me. She was a hand-fashioned doll named Precious Belle, made especially for me. I still have her and love her. She is now twenty-nine years old.

I thought I was done with my Christmas adventure, but still more people had heard about our efforts and came asking for my help. I was able to continue to come up with gifts, though not as personalized as the others.

As I left the church, an older, African-American lady approached me. It seemed she had been waiting at the church, hoping we would return there, in order to ask if, by any chance, I had one more doll she could give to her granddaughter. I was glad I could tell her that I did have a pretty one left, but that she was a white doll.

"Oh, that is perfect," she said. "Just what my granddaughter wished for!"

So we went back inside the church and wrapped our last doll in pretty Christmas paper. I hugged a happy grandmother, who was hugging her granddaughter's gift, and we wished each other a merry Christmas.

However, still more help was requested! Two ladies from Pompano Beach Social Services came to me asking if I could possibly help find a baby crib for one of their young families whose newborn baby was sleeping in a cardboard box.

We asked around among our loyal friends and supporters, and found a fully appointed, beautiful crib. How generous of a family to pass on a crib to a less fortunate family at Christmas time! That little baby did not have to sleep in a cardboard box anymore. It reminded me of the baby that was born in a manger and was the reason for Christmas. We said, "Thank you, God!"

After that, we were surprised and a little dismayed to see an article in the Pompano Beach paper about my being able to find the baby a crib. The supervisor of the two employees who had called me to see if I could find a crib let it be known that their asking for my help was not necessary and was uncalled for because that was the Social Services Department's job and I did not work for Social Services.

That article upset many helpers and supporters. I assured them that what really mattered, though, was that a needy little baby no longer had to sleep in a box.

Jim and I felt our job was over when the last gift had been given. Our Christmas was spent going to Christmas Eve services at our church and thanking God for making it possible for us to help so many and spread the joy of Christmas and the glory of the birth of Jesus Christ to all those needy children and their parents and grandparents.

These are the kinds of Christmases one never forgets. We repeated our Christmas gift-giving efforts for several more years with the same generous responses from the public, until we moved back to Colorado in 1986. Still, those Christmases in Florida had made up more of my unbelievable adventures!

CHAPTER 34:

The Baby Laurel Adventure

Young Jacqueline's marriage was on the rocks. She and her husband were totally mismatched and she had a hard time living with Ben.

Ben was a macho man who attracted her with his sex appeal and who needed to talk down to her all the time to make up for the differences in their intelligence. Maybe she did not know any better since she grew up with a father who treated her, her sister, and me the same way. Fortunately, we did not get "beaten down"—just the opposite happened. We became very strong women and, without a doubt, overachievers.

Jacqueline, a very bright young lady, had earned her college degree, maintaining a 4.0 grade point average. Ben had no schooling but was a good foreign automobile mechanic. They had nothing in common other than attraction and, eventually, even that fell through. She thought having a child maybe would improve or save their marriage, but it did not change things other than making Jacque's decision to get a divorce easier.

Jacqueline decided an immediate divorce would be best for all concerned. She shouldered the burden and responsibility of bringing up their sweet eight-month-old little daughter, Laurel, by herself. Ben did not pay any child support.

Jim and I invited her to come and stay with us for a while until she could decide what her and Laurel's future should look like. She arrived at our house in a little Volkswagen Rabbit with a baby crib strapped on the top. Laurel was in a baby seat and the big, beautiful German shepherd dog, Sabel, was in the front seat. She drove like the wind all the way from Eugene, Oregon, to Florida in two days.

Laurel and I bouncing on the new miniature rampoline

It was a delightful gift for us to see little Laurel grow up. Jim, or "Opa" (which means "grandfather") took over the male role in Laurel's life. While the two of them stayed with us the first few months, he would be the one to get up and comfort her or walk her at night when she was fussy or ill. Laurel took her first steps in our house.

We enjoyed having the four of us together. Laurel, who is now the mother of a little boy named Strummer and a daughter Everly Grace is still close due to the telephone, the computer and daily photographs. It is our pleasure to share many precious moments with her.

Broward Tribune
October 13, 1981

Bouncing grandma wins

Grandmother Ingeborg Johnston, owner of To Your Good Health, a nutrition and fitness store in Pompano Beach, received the grand prize and a letter of appreciation from the American Heart Association for earning over $800 for the association by bouncing four hours on a rebound unit in a contest sponsored by the School of Rhythmic Bounce-Exercise and hosted by the Sportsrooms of Fort Lauderdale.

Mrs. Johnston, called "Super Mouse" by her friends, out-pointed 25 younger men and women in collecting the largest amount of pledges and money.

The doctor-supervised event, lasted from 8:00 a.m. until 5:00 p.m. and was the first charity event of its kind. Approximately $3,000.00 was earned by the competitors for the Broward County American Heart Association.

The grand prize was a two year membership to the Sportsrooms and a bounce-exerciser received from the School of Rhythmic Bounce-Exercise which Mrs. Johnston donated to charity.

Grandma bouncing her way to victory

CHAPTER 35:

Founding a National Hug Holiday Almost Though We did Collect Over 1,000,000 Hugs One Year

How many times have you been asked, "Would you like a refill?" and never thought a lot about it?

As I mentioned previously, Florida had a large population of single, older people, many with handicaps, who lived alone—not always by choice, but often through circumstances. These individuals rarely got the opportunity to be touched or especially to be hugged in a loving way by anyone. That fact creates a multitude of conditions, a few of which are: poor appetite, poor eating habits, loss of energy, overall fatigue, and, many times, even depression.

In my counseling sessions connected to our health food store, I always started asking my clients how they felt at that moment, and how they coped during the past week. I also questioned if they had eaten breakfast, lunch, or whatever meal was closest to the time of their appointment. Also what did they eat? How much did they eat? No one seemed to connect eating, food, and good or bad nutrition with their well-being. This was the early 1980s.

I was never surprised by the answers I got but was always prepared to offer a bowl or cup of my powerful vegetable or chicken soup, which my clients gladly accepted. The soup became popular and very much appreciated. It did help them realize how much better they felt after counseling and having had nourishment for the body at the same time.

I never let them leave without getting a hug and reminding them that Jim and I "gave refills!" We could count on them coming by just to get their "refill" of hugs and perhaps also a bowl of soup.

It seemed such a little gesture of caring to people who were "huggers" by nature to give comfort to another person. Just imagine if you would never get a hug again. Coming from a "hugging" family and having a "hugging" husband, I would just wither away without my hugs.

Over time, Jim and I earned a widespread reputation in South Florida with all our hugging, and as the praise of its benefits kept spreading, we became well known. Jim's graduate degree in educational psychology, I am sure, prompted all of this! The news media picked up on it and asked if they could cover our hugging experiences.

Jim thought it was about time that we created a "Hug Holiday." So we did. Seeing the great need all around us, we just kept spreading good will and hugging people. We continued with our hugging on a special day we called the Hug Holiday.

The Broward County Sentinel was the first newspaper to assign a reporter and photography team to follow us for three years on our "Hug Day" in order to document and report the reaction and willingness of people to hug or be hugged.

We went to nursing homes, some fancy and expensive, some adequate—but the most heart-wrenching ones were the state-run nursing homes. We hugged people there who *never* received visitors, who had no families to look after them, and who were just begging for attention. Most of them were in wheelchairs, and, between Jim and me, we were hugging most of the people in a bent-over position all day long. It became quite tiring.

At six-three, Jim was on his knees most of the time and by the end of the day, his beaten-up "basketball knees" had a hard time functioning properly. Sometimes he had to be helped to get off the floor. But to see the grateful faces and the reaching hands to touch made all of our efforts more meaningful and gratifying.

The photographer who was, at first, skeptical about the value of hugging, and very reluctantly followed us around to shoot photographs. During the third year, however, a lady in a wheelchair pointed to him, saying, "I want a hug from him." Jim and I thought, *Oh, no, now what?*

Jim and I practicing what we do best, enjoying each other

You should have seen him! We could not believe it! He proceeded to sling the many cameras that were dangling on his chest over his head and on to the floor. Once clear of his paraphernalia, he just marched over to her, got on his knees, and gave her the biggest hug she ever had!

We felt we had arrived! We reached our goal at that very moment, when he hugged that lady, by having as many people, even the skeptical ones, involved in hugging other people as we could possibly manage.

It was a wonderful sight to see this hardened, "seen and photographed it all" reporting photographer feel the gratitude radiating from that lady. It brought tears to his eyes. I am not wrong when I say that young man was never the same again. He had unknowingly learned something about compassion and love.

We were told by our reporter and her photographer that they had kept count and we hugged approximately 900+ people that day.

It was always a special time for the residents of the nursing homes when we brought children into their lives. When appropriate, we would invite classes of kindergarteners and their teachers to come and help us hug. Jim would ask the assembled kids, "Do you know what a hug is?" Oh, yes, they knew. He asked them to show him. One of the little ones just took a running leap right into his arms and gave him the biggest hug he could manage.

The children went to every one of the residents and hugged them. It did not matter to them if they could not reach the person in the wheelchair; they just hugged the knees and the wheelchair. Whatever they could reach was being hugged.

One time, in one of the more expensive beautiful nursing homes, my tall husband approached a very distinguished-looking lady sitting in her wheelchair; with her hands clasped in her lap and her head tilted down, she was a very serene picture.

Jim thinks people in wheelchairs don't get enough hugs, simply because it's awkward. He does not mind and makes special efforts in that direction. So he got down on his knees and asked her, "May I have a hug?"

She lifted her head and Jim looked into the most beautiful blue eyes he had ever seen. It was apparent that her mind was clouded. As Jim hugged her, you could just see it coming into her eyes that she remembered that pleasant feeling. He said, "Thank you" and, as he left, looked back and saw her smiling as she put her head down again and went back into herself.

The media continued picking up the Hug Holiday activities nationwide, and their reporting about the various events focused more and more on us.

Churches contacted us, pledging large amounts of hugs from their congregations. The Alcoholics Anonymous Association pledged large amounts of hugs at their conventions. We had contests created among various nursing homes, pledging hugs. We were presented with final counts mounted on pretty displays. It was getting bigger and bigger and we just could not devote the time required by the volume of mail and calls, so we decided to turn our information over to an interested organization. They promoted it for a while then it apparently died since we did not hear from them or about them anymore.

Jim and I moved to Denver in 1986 and continued our hugging on a smaller scale in the Mile High City. We again had reporters follow us as we hugged in front of large health food stores, in malls, and in downtown Denver on the main street.

On that busy street, my husband asked a young lady who looked like she had the world in her hand for a hug. Not only was she beautiful, but she was also looking every bit the successful executive that she was. No doubt the world was her oyster!

As she hugged Jim, she broke out in tears and sobbed, "You have no idea how badly I needed that hug! Thank you so very much for it." You never know what kind of burden people are carrying around with them.

It seemed that out of every ten people we hugged, one or two would break down and cry, thanking us for our thoughtfulness. It made us sad that there was so much need, but glad that we could serve and comfort some of the needy, hurting souls.

Jim and I still hug and get hugged in return. When we are greeters at our Methodist church, we hug everyone coming in the door. The need and longing for that touch and its comfort is there, quietly hidden, but it is there, waiting for someone to waken and fulfill it.

Please make a point of looking around you at the widows and widowers you meet in your daily life. Try to see the loss they are carrying daily and the effect of that loss that will never go away. Offer them a hug and enjoy their happy response. It will make them feel good—and you too.

I am challenging you, my readers, to create your own adventures and perform random "acts of kindness." The opportunities are all around you. Look for them! You will find that the rewards you receive in return are overwhelming!

CHAPTER 36:

Helmut Coming to America from
East Berlin for My Sixtieth Birthday

When Helmut wrote to me expressing his hope that he could come to America to visit and to celebrate my sixtieth birthday with us in 1984, Jim and I could hardly believe it. He told us if we mailed him a fully paid, round-trip ticket on a Communist country airline, it would be possible. Imagine my joy just at the possibility alone!

We purchased a ticket for him on a Czechoslovakian airline; he would have to fly from Berlin to Prague and on to New York, where I'd pick him up and take him to our home in Pompano Beach, Florida. He could have flown from West Berlin but that was not allowed since it would surely not bring any dollars into the Communist block.

He carried the ticket in his back pocket, wearing it to shreds by showing it to friends and customers. When he told people in Berlin that he was flying to America, they replied, "Sure, you are!" Nobody believed Helmut until he showed them his ticket.

Before receiving his passport and the official permit to leave, he and his wife were investigated by the infamous East German "Volpo: Many friends, neighbors in his apartment house, customers, and vendors were interrogated to see if they thought he would defect! While that is impossible to believe in this country, it was a simple fact in East Berlin. Everyone interrogated would have been accused and would have faced punishment had he defected! Something as simple as being "questioned" on behalf of someone else was already alarming, unwelcome, and dreaded by the average citizen.

Because of Helmut's status as a disabled or handicapped person, the authorities were inclined to let him leave East Berlin. He was expendable! Other conditions included that he would lose his pension, property, and business if he did not return. His wife, who was younger and more physically fit, was not expendable so she was not permitted to leave. But she would have lost everything had *he* not returned!

Helmut told us that when he left Berlin and the plane lifted off on the way to Prague, his dream to see his sister in America was actually happening. When the plane to New York lifted off the runway from Prague, he held his breath for quite a while, thinking, *If they do not call this plane back, I am going to make it.* Thank God!

Never will I forget my anticipation of being able to welcome my brother to America. That possibility had not even entered my mind.

For the date of his planned arrival, I had flown to New York from Florida and was waiting at the international airport waiting room for many hours while Helmut was going through immigration. I was waiting and hoping, not knowing if he had really been on the expected plane.

When I finally saw him coming toward me, it was an overwhelming experience for both of us! All he could say repeatedly was, "Inge, do you believe this? Can you really believe that I am here? Here, in New York?"

We stayed in New York and did some sightseeing. We visited places he had dreamed about, like the Statue of Liberty, the famous graffiti-painted subways, Times Square, and, of course, we walked on Broadway. We took a boat ride to and around the Statue of Liberty, which was cloaked in scaffolding for renovation and did not receive visitors. But she still looked majestic and beautiful as we extended our respects to her. The boat ride was a glorious experience and its lasting memory was taken back by Helmut to the dreary prison-confinement-like-life in East Berlin.

Helmut and I just sat happily in that tour boat with our arms linked, looking around and enjoying every minute of that trip. Every so often, of course, we'd say, "Do you believe this?"

He admired Times Square and when we walked along Broadway, he kept saying, "Inge, do you realize we are walking on history?" I just had to reply, "That's not *all* we're walking on!" I thought Broadway was really dirty.

When Helmut saw and experienced the famous subways, he just glowed. He and I were born in Berlin, so you could not say he was a visitor from a little, hick town. But he loved New York, with all the lively bustle and noise. The skyscrapers caused him to walk endlessly with his head up. He was overwhelmed by all of the love and friendliness extended to him, as well as by the beauty of the sea of lights and the many, many cars.

Part of my brother's dream was to see Florida, and that, too, was happening. We drove to Cape Canaveral and took the offered tour; as a bonus, he saw the Columbia space shuttle sitting on the tarmac, having been scheduled for a space shot shortly after we left. He kept whispering in awe, "Inge, look how close we are to it." Being free, not shackled by guards, police, or spies—just free—was the experience of a lifetime for him!

Obviously, life in East Berlin behind the wall was quite different. In America, he ate corn on the cob and spare ribs using his fingers, a practice not common in Germany. He had a super-sundae and loved it. But his favorite food was prime rib. I bought him his last prime rib dinner at the airport in New York before his departure back to East Berlin. I tried to talk him into taking a prime rib sandwich to his wife, Helga, but he was afraid it would be taken away going through customs and would cause trouble for him.

Helmut had also expressed the wish to see San Francisco, so he and I flew there on a big plane that was ultimately destined for Hawaii. He was impressed by its size, comfort, and décor. He sat in a window seat, with just one seat next to him; we were served filet mignon—and this was coach class! But that was 1984, and that's the way it was.

We took a tour bus to see the San Francisco sights. He thought the Golden Gate Bridge was truly a beauty. The guide on the bus asked everyone where they were from, and the other passengers were delighted when they heard that Helmut came from behind the Iron Curtain and was enjoying California.

We had to chuckle when everyone had guessed that we were new-lyweds. He told them, "I lost my heart in San Francisco" and got a big round of applause! It was a delight to show him Fisherman's Wharf and eat there.

Jim and I were grateful that we could offer all of that to Helmut. We took a lot of photographs that went back to East Berlin to be shown to his friends and customers.

Helmut had a relatively happy life in retirement until in 1988 he developed prostate cancer. He died several days after the Berlin Wall came down. I talked to him during his final days and asked if he knew the Berlin Wall had collapsed. He said yes a dream had come true but that it was too late for him. He died several days after the collapse. He was buried in Berlin.

Years later after my brother's death Jim wrote a tribute to him.
The Spirit of the Berlin Wall and a Life Celebration of Helmut Balendat
November 1989

As the Berlin Wall came crashing down, the Spirit of Freedom, in the dark and ugly cold for some thirty years, awoke, unfolded like butterfly's wings, blinked at the lights, heard noises long silenced and was awed by excited crowds. It ascended to that place in the sky where all spirits go when they are released from their earthly bonds.

Over the years the Wall snaked through Central Europe, in some places extremely formidable, in others a mere wire fence. It divided not only the countryside but families, a common culture and even the world.

As the wounds caused by the Wall heal and the Spirit of the Wall lifts to the sky, it is joined by other spirits, one recently departed from a body racked with pain from the ravages of cancer.

We thank you, Lord, for releasing the Spirit of Freedom., I do not have to speak to the importance of this event, for millions whose lives have changed forever are doing that now and far more eloquently than I.

I speak for the spirit that is all that is left of a man who lived in troubled times.

World War II robbed him of his youth.

As a World War II Russian prisoner of war, he was robbed of his old age.

He was robbed of his happiness instead of being rewarded for his success in building a family business that would have made him a millionaire certainly in America and even in West Berlin.

He was robbed of the exhilaration and pleasure that go with doing the impossible well, because of harsh Communist rules and regulations.

He was robbed of his right to work freely as a master craftsman of his trade.

His was not that part of Germany whose economic base was reestablished by generous Americans with their Marshall Plan.

His was that part of Germany where the entire economic base not destroyed was robbed by Russia and removed to that country under the concept of "spoils of war."

He was robbed of that part of his intellect that watched Western television, where individual freedoms were taken for granted, living in a culture absent of individual freedoms.

He was an intellectual with class, forced to live in a classless society.

This man's spirit deserves your special attention, Lord. In spite of all that was taken away from him or perhaps because of it, the world will be a better place and those who know him will be better for their relationship with him.

He had a tough, unfair life. The challenges he overcame would have overwhelmed all but the strongest here in the United States.

He always worked hard and came out at least even in the face of long odds and an extremely uncaring government.

But You know all that, Lord. You know how loving and supportive his sister was. She carried suitcases hundred of times filled with toilet paper and other hard-to-find supplies into East Berlin. She knew the Berlin Wall and "Checkpoint Charlie" as well as any civilian could. Year after year, she supplied the Balendat family with goods not available anywhere in the Eastern Block countries, and she made those trips happily from America to Berlin.

We know that You would not put Helmut through these trials and tribulations without a reason and that You do not have to share that reason with us.

But whatever it is You ask of his spirit, it will be completed the only way he knew how. It would be done on time, absolutely and meticulously correct and complete in every detail.

James R. Johnston, Brother-in-Law
November 1989

CHAPTER 37:

When the Berlin Wall was Breached, East Berliners Stormed into West Berlin asking, "Where Am I?"

The infamous Berlin Wall was breached on September 9, 1989. The young people born in East Berlin between 1960 and 1989, along with their friends and relatives, flooded through the openings in the wall into West Berlin and other areas of West Germany, having no idea where they were or where they were going. They had no concept of the section of Berlin they were in and didn't know the names of the streets they were walking on, yet they were only a few blocks from where they lived in East Berlin all their lives.

Who could imagine what it felt like walking around with a map that they had been using for years, showing East Berlin and Eastern Germany in great detail, but that was blank, totally blank, beyond the wall that separated Germany, including Berlin, into two parts?

The Communists had perfected the isolation of their population to unbelievable degrees. East Berliners entered a different world when they set foot on Western soil.

The joy of unification was great, but, as time passed, it became a big headache for most unhappy people who had been separated and had become estranged from family and friends for twenty-nine years. The East Germans expected to be treated like the West Germans, and the West Germans thought them to be a tremendous burden. Even to this day, it remains a challenging problem.

The original "Check Point Charlie" the only gate in the Berlin Wall where diplomats and foreigners could pass through from West Berlin to East Berlin and back.

CHAPTER 38:

*Granddaughter Laurel Visits Her
Great-Grandfather's Village in
Eastern Germany Near the Polish Border*

As a graduation gift, Jim and I took our granddaughter, Laurel (Jacqueline's daughter), on a three-week vacation to Germany in 1989. We flew to Frankfurt and on to Berlin. What a joy it was to see my friend Uschi and her friend Helmut at the Tempelhof Airport, welcoming us to Berlin. It was our nineteen-year-old granddaughter's first trip to Germany and she was awed by it all.

My best friend Uschi, whom I've known since we both were six years old, had nursed me through every visit behind the Iron Curtain. She welcomed Laurel with the same love and hospitality she had extended to me all those years when I visited my family behind the Berlin Wall.

We stayed at a bed and breakfast near Uschi's apartment, which in itself was a delight for Laurel. We went sightseeing the next day, taking a Berlin tour bus with an English commentary, which Laurel and Jim listened to with earphones. It was an informative and delightful experience for both of them. We, of course, had to see the famous Berlin Zoo, but the highlight for Laurel, after having seen all the famous buildings and museums, was the "Kurfuersten Damm," the fashion center and the must-see street of Berlin. She thought that the bombed-out

Gedaechtnis Kirche (Memorial Church), with its modern addition called "the Lipstick" by Berliners because of its shape, was really imposing.

We took a boat ride, called a "Dampfer Fahrt," through the many waterways around Berlin and the areas where I grew up. Having seen all of Berlin's notable attractions, we rented a car and drove an hour or so into East Germany. Laurel was touched to see the little village of Alt Tucheband and my grandparents' house. After having heard all the stories of my vacations spent there with my Oma and Opa, (my grandparents) it was so much more meaningful when I could actually point out and describe where everything happened and what it used to look like!

It was sad for me that Laurel only got to see the war-torn and totally demolished little village. But my grandfather's big stalwart house was still there, as imposing as ever, with the effects of the fierce fighting still showing the war wounds and bullet holes inflicted in 1945 by defending German troops and the advancing Russian troops. (The Russian soldiers were on their way to the big, coveted prize: Berlin!)

After the war was over, the Communists confiscated the grand house and converted it into eight crude apartments and the former stables into eight garages. It broke my heart! I hadn't seen it since the Iron Curtain had gone up. I did not make an effort to go inside the house and look.

CHAPTER 39:

*German-to-English Translations for German
Nobel Prize Nominee Hans Nieper, M.D.*

When I met Dr. Nieper professionally at a health food convention, he asked me if I would be interested in translating a book for him from German-to-English. A second book was to be translated after the first one was completed. Dr. Nieper was a distinguished medical doctor and a renowned oncologist known all over the world, and I was overwhelmed to be considered for such an honor.

When I was in Berlin, I researched and purchased several medical dictionaries to take back to America with me, preparing for these translations. It was my pleasure and I was able to translate the books successfully. Being bilingual and a retired nurse made me a natural for the job because some medical knowledge was essential to do his book justice.

I was invited to visit Dr. Hans. A. Nieper and welcomed to his home in Hanover, Germany, regarding the translation of his book, *Revolution in Technology, Medicine and Society*. When I flew into Hanover and arrived at the airport gate, I was surprised to see Dr. Nieper and his wife welcoming me and holding a big sign with my name on it, fearing they might miss me.

I spent two days with them and had the honor of being lectured to by Dr. Nieper personally on his various inventive supplements and the special formulas to be given by injection. His early research instilled his certainty that cancer therapy using "poisonous cytostate substances" (which had been practiced then and even now) was predominantly on the wrong track.

As an internist, through his investigations and research (together with those of a well-known German chemist), he discovered and developed various health curatives, including certain "mineral carriers" such as aspartates, orotates, arginates and 2-AEP. Those unknowledgeable in the fields of nutrition would not have much appreciation for these advancements. However, Dr. Nieper discovered what is now the only medication officially declared in Germany to be effective against multiple sclerosis.

His extensive study of non-poisonous methods for the long-term treatment of cancer made him a star witness for American Health Choice Freedom organizations, of which our store was one, opposing toxic "orthodox" medicine and government therapy regulation.

I could go on and on about this man's contributions, like introducing Potassium and Magnesium Aspartates into heart therapy, the routine introduction of selenium therapy for heart protection, the value of using pineapple enzymes and beta-carotene against cancer, and the concept that the best defense against cancer involves both immune defense and gene repair.

Jim and I have been most interested and involved in the Health Knowledge Revolution that has taken place somewhere between 1950 and now. We provided important leadership in helping others understand how health knowledge has been made available to all because of today's high technology, internet and computer age we enjoy. The instant and infinite information now available provides unlimited possibilities never before available. The material Dr. Nieper makes available in his book is an example of what information is available to all who are interested.

Jim and my efforts in developing the CN Certified Nutritionist education and professional credentialing program started a new profession in the natural foods and products industries as well as the alternative, complementary and functional health care industries. A second start-up profession for Jim my first. Constant roadblocks thrown-up by traditional health care communities has only made us stronger. Because of our contribution in education and professionalism in these fields we are in touch with many others who made and are making outstanding contributions in this area.

Emmanual Cheraskin, M.D., Inge Johnston CN (Certified Nutritionst) and Lyle Smith, M.D, all pioneers of the natural food industry's spearhead toward professionalism through education and credentialing

CHAPTER 40:

Bringing to America New German-to-English Book Translations,
for Nobel Prize Nominee Johanna Budwig, Ph.D.

Jim and I visited Dr. Johanna Budwig at her home in Southern Germany. She was a nominee for the Nobel Prize a number of times and famous for her nutrition books and diets.

We had the opportunity to discuss her work at great length, and I agreed to translate several of her books from German-to-English.

Graciously, she insisted on giving me numerous copies of her books to take home with me. Several of them have her personal notations in them. I am probably the only person in the country who has a complete library of the books that she has written.

She advocated a mixture of freshly pressed flaxseed oil and "Quark," a refined German cottage cheese, to be the best combination and main ingredient of her dietary suggestions. The fat in the Quark combined with the protein in the flax seed bypassed the liver and went directly into the blood stream. Jim and I brought her flaxseed oil and Quark concept back to America in 1986 and discussed it with our professional friends in the natural foods and products industries. We wrote a thirty-page booklet about the value of the process and the Omega-3 flaxseed oil, which was distributed to various industries around the world.

Dr. Johanna Budwig and I at her home in Freudenstadt, Germany

Clients came from all over the world for consultations with Dr. Budwig, and she was successful in treating not just one affliction, but many different illnesses. She was quite a lady, having fought the margarine industry when she began her professional life, providing evidence of the detrimental effects of margarine products on the health of the German population.

We brought Dr. Budwig's concepts to America and after making many presentations around the country we put the Omega-3 fats information into the minds of thousands including some individuals and companies who have carried our flag successfully with this information.

Ordinarily, in Germany, special tax breaks are made available to citizens that make such important social contributions. However, Jim was not able to intervene successfully on her behalf to the German Internal Revenue Service regarding the contributions she made.

CHAPTER 41:

*My Aerial Combat Training Experience
in a T-34 at the Age of 79!*

There's a bogie on my tail! I am taking evasive action!

Just tell me, what would a nice, seventy-nine-year-old lady (at least I think I deserve to be called a "lady") know about "Bogies" and "Evasive Action"? Let me explain how I was introduced to this and quickly learned all about it.

My very loving, considerate husband was running out of unusual anniversary gifts for me. He had previously given me sailplane rides, balloon rides, scuba-diving trips on various barrier reefs, including the Great Barrier Reef in Australia, and unusual diamond jewelry, including blue and green diamonds. What else was there?

Well, would you believe that this time, in June 2002, for our twenty-fifth anniversary, he gave me the gift of a T-34 aerial combat training course conducted by the Sky Fighters, Inc. at the Centennial Airport in Englewood, Colorado! The instructors were highly decorated retired war heroes, conducting these classes out of love of flying—and especially flying the T-34.

Getting ready to take off in the T 34. Jim flew the same model plane in Navy flight training fifty six years ago.

When Jim had received his degree and commission in the Navy in 1956, he began flight training in Pensacola, Florida. He trained in the T-34 and was fond of that small, low-wing plane. The T-34 was widely used for training pilots in the Navy as well as in the Air Force. Many foreign countries still use that model plane.

Knowing and nurturing my adventurous spirit whenever he could, he was sure I would like the aerial combat training course and enjoy the experience. When he surprised me with that fantastic gift, I asked him what he would have done if I said I did not want to learn aerial combat training. He just laughed and replied, "It never dawned on me."

When we got to the airport, the Sky Fighter instructors thought Jim was the one about to fly and were pretty astounded that I was the one! They did not get many female candidates and certainly not anyone my age.

My instructor was an Air Force Academy graduate and a retired Air Force colonel whose call name was "Gunbow," which he had used while serving several tours flying in Vietnam. We got along just fine and I got a hug from him coming and going. Age does have its privileges!

I was introduced to my "opponent," a young man in his twenties who had been up in the T-34 before. We started out by fitting me into a jumpsuit, gloves, and helmet, and I was furnished with a helmet bag. I was surprised that they had a suit to fit me, being just five feet tall, but it sure made it less complicated.

I needed a call name and my husband chose "Tiger." We had an extensive briefing; Jim sat in on it and let it bring back memories. We learned in theory maneuvers like high yoyos, low yoyos, rolls, loops, victory rolls, and evasive actions.

Then off we went to the plane. I just knew and anticipated that my height and size would be a problem, but I learned to live with it and compensate for it. When I put my parachute on, it reached the top of my neck, meeting the lower part of my helmet, and went all the way down to the bottom of my seat. The seat itself had to be brought forward as far as it could and had to be raised to its maximum height. Still, I had to sit up very straight to be able to see my gun sight in the windshield. My instructor was checking on me to make sure I was safe overall and safely strapped in.

As Gunbow acquainted me with the plane and gave me safety instructions, he told me to be careful if, in an emergency, I had to get out of the plane in flight. "Climb out onto the wing and jump, but be sure to get away from the fuselage before deploying the parachute," he said.

Having parachuted before, the thought of jumping did not bother me. My concern was how to climb out on the wing of an airplane in distress (and most likely in an awkward position or maybe even spiraling), being fully outfitted and with the parachute hindering my movements and making it awkward for me to get out of the cockpit and get onto the wing.

I paid attention to all he told me. When he was done, I asked him to do me a favor in case of an emergency: "Please, if at all possible, turn the plane upside down and I will do my best and just fall out!" Gunbow thought that was very funny.

The T-34 is a two-seater plane; I sat in the front seat with the instructor behind me. We had an open intercom in our helmets and could talk freely. When Gunbow talked to the air controllers, I listened to everything he said. I fell in love with that plane and wanted to take it home with me but was told that they still needed it. How narrow-minded! Oh, well!

Our two planes lined up and got into position for takeoff. Because of traffic around the airport, we got permission to take off and were assigned air space in which to do our aerial maneuvers. It was just wonderful—flying along and having only the thin, clear canopy between me and the wide, beautiful heavens! I felt that was the closest

I could come to God and not have to die. I had flown before in little high-wing planes, but not in a low-wing one. I will forever prefer the low-wing plane!

We arrived at our assigned air space and proceeded with our maneuvers. I was thrilled when he told me to "Take the plane." I did. What a shock! The "stick" is so unbelievably sensitive that when I took it the first time and really grabbed and muscled it, the plane responded immediately by going all over the place: up, down, and sideways. I could not believe it!

When I told Jim about that traumatic response afterwards, he just laughed. He and his fellow novices in 1956 had the same response! They were told to grab the stick with two fingers from the top and control it that way. I could not do that because I had a bomb release button and a gun button on the top of the stick.

On the way home after that first class, I stopped at a computer store to purchase a aerial combat game and started practicing with "Messerschmitt" and "Spitfire" planes. I was not going back and disgracing myself again.

It paid off. After the next takeoff, when asked to take control of the plane, I could hold it perfectly in position and maneuver it with competence. I was so proud of myself as the wingman! When I was going along beautifully and settling down to business, I looked for my lead and saw him way above and ahead of me.

I asked Gunbow, "What is he doing up there?" He replied calmly, "Nothing. What are we doing down here?"

Boy, I got going, caught up with him, and took my "wingman" position. I sure could find more ways to make me feel dumb.

As we went along, things got better and I did pretty well. I kept shooting and hitting my opponent (who would release smoke whenever he perceived I hit the target). Gunbow would shout, "Tiger, you got him! Stay on him. You can get him again and again!"

After shooting and hitting him the first time, my reaction was one of awe. In that moment, however, my opponent tried to get away. I caught on fast, my competitive nature kicked in, and I "got" him many more times! What fun when I was asked to do a victory roll again and again!

I was lucky in my maneuvers and ended up behind my opponent, causing his instructor to call out, "I have a bogie on my tail!" and "Take evasive action!" I did shoot him down again after that and did another victory roll to show my pleasure!

At the debriefing afterwards, it was mentioned that my actions were supposed to have been executed at the *next* training level and that I "had jumped the gun," so to speak. Fortunately, they did not ask me to explain my maneuver and how I got behind them. I really didn't know how I did that. Just lucky, I guess.

I was proud when I got my certificate of completion for the first level in aerial combat training. I flew the last time in January 2003, just a few months before we moved to Oak Harbor, Washington.

Oak Harbor has a flying club at the Navy base airport and two T-34s are parked there. One of them is a newer model with a three-bladed propeller, compared to the model I flew with just two blades. Jim and I go by there occasionally to visit "my plane."

That aerial combat training course was a gift that keeps on giving to me! It was another one of my many adventures that I keep remembering and reliving often and with real pleasure. Especially when I'm lying in bed before going to sleep, I bring back the wonderful sensation of flying—the fantastic freedom of moving that little plane at my will in the beauty of the endless sky.

I will be forever grateful to Jim and his continuous thoughtfulness. He understands and nourishes my adventurous spirit. And what an unbelievable adventure it was—aerial combat training in the same model airplane Jim flew fifty years before.

CHAPTER 42:

*Young or Old, Make Acts of Kindness
a Vital Part of Your Live*

My aerial combat lessons are a good place to close this book. I do so reminding you to put more Acts of Kindness in your life. You can do that at any age. Why? Because the more we perform the Acts of Kindness the nicer the world becomes.

A the time of writing this book I am an active 86 year old lady. We have an eighty-eight-year-old neighbor, Helen, who called us one morning at 6:00 a.m., asking if we could taking her to the Naval Air Station Hospital in Oak Harbor, Washington, because she was having chest pains. Since Jim is a retired Navy Captain, he is able to go on the base anytime so we were able to take her there at once.

At the time, Helen was the sole caretaker of her invalid, bedridden husband, Don, who had Alzheimer's. Friends living nearby were hurriedly called and asked to stay with her husband while we took her to the Navy base.

The doctors at the hospital stabilized Helen, but were not equipped to keep her at the base and transferred her to Whidbey General Hospital in Coupeville, Washington. That left us and their two friends to take care of her and her bedridden husband. We two couples were not able to do that.

It took some unbelievable efforts on our part, trying to have Don, a much-decorated Navy veteran looked after. Among his many military achievements, he was a "Silver Eagle," a senior pilot who had been qualified to fly twenty-five different airplanes and helicopters during World War II as an enlisted man!

Now, here he was, alone in his Alzheimer-ridden condition, lying helplessly in bed. We tried to explain to him what happened to his wife, who we were, and that we were making arrangements for him to be taken care of, but he could not understand. We did not want him being ripped out of bed by medics and taken away by ambulance without at least trying to provide some sort of explanation.

We called 911 and when the ambulance responded, the medics came rushing into the house, carrying all their emergency equipment. But they did not find an "emergency." They found an old gentleman lying in bed, looking at them calmly. They considered it a false alarm and were getting ready to leave. It took an hour-long conversation between me and a hospital official to get permission to transport him to the hospital where his wife had already been admitted.

I kept telling the medics and the individual on the phone that since the other couple had to leave and I could not stay (let alone handle Don by myself, even if I could stay), it should be considered an emergency because, in fact, it was one. I won and they did declare it an emergency.

The medics took him to the hospital, where he was "parked" in a corner of the emergency room until an assisted Alzheimer home in Oak Harbor could be found that agreed to admit him. It took a lot more effort to locate a more suitable and permanent home for him, which we helped to find, and he died in comfort three months later. Mr. and Mrs. Hammer, the good friends of our troubled neighbors for some forty-five years, helped Helen go into an assisted living home two years after her husband died.

What all of these efforts go to show is that would not be much of a civilization without being aware of the value of such acts of kindness, which somehow change both the giver and the receiver.

My adventures never end nor should yours. No matter how old you are or what the circumstances are or the kind of challenges you face, seek adventures helping others!

I am a collector of Acts of Kindness. Do you have some you would like to share with me?

Young or old make Acts of Kindness an Important Part of Your Life.

1. Join AoK (Acts of Kindness)Central

*An international organization
formed to make the world a
little nicer place to live in*

2. Requirement:

*Agree to perform one
Act of Kindness daily*

3. Action

*email me at Inge@AOK Central.org
a short story about how an Act of
Kindness changed a life for the better,
yours or someone else's*

INDEX

V

W

Possible List of Adventures for Next Book

1. Joined German folk dance group with Jim in Denver. Danced all over the state and spent two weeks in Germany dancing with various groups.
2. Adventures in "Gift-giving" and "taking," including the Blue Diamond affair
3. Helping "Chancy," our friendly horse neighbor
4. The Blue Moon Motel adventure
5. Walking backwards down one of Germany's best-known mountains
6. Winning garden club honors with flower arrangements as a beginner
7. Stories from counseling days, including, "I have the best doctors…"
8. Birthdays, including the one in Germany when I sat on the stairs, waiting
9. Winning Arthur Murray Dancing contest with Jim
10. Problem with U.S. Coast Guard about value of U.S. Passsport
11. Cooking so no one knows it's good for them
12. Raising funds for needy projects, something unknown in Germany
13. Examples of life-long passions helping people, animals and plants grow
14. My first glider ride with Jim
15. Kayaking around Berlin as a youth
16. World War Two boy friends
17. Motorcycling with Jim in the Colorado Mountains
18. PTA efforts supporting daughters Eileen and Jacqueline
19. Taking on Nazi Officials to get shoes for my mother